David K. Faux

Understanding Ontario First Nations Genealogical Records Sources and Case Studies

Toronto
The Ontario Genealogical Society

Further copies of this book and information about the Society can be obtained by writing to:

The Ontario Genealogical Society
Suite 102, 40 Orchard View Boulevard
Toronto ON M4R 1B9
Canada

National Library of Canada Cataloguing in Publication

Faux, David Kenneth, 1947–

Understanding Ontario First Nations genealogical records : sources and cases / by David K. Faux.

Includes bibliographical references and index
ISBN 0-7779-2121-9

1. Indians of North America – Ontario – Genealogy.
I. Ontario Genealogical Society   II. Title.

E98.G44F38 2002   929'.3'089970713   C2002-901569-3

Cover designed by University of Toronto Press

Printed by University of Toronto Press

Published by The Ontario Genealogical Society
Suite 102, 40 Orchard View Boulevard
Toronto ON M4R 1B9
Canada
ogs@bellnet.ca
www.ogs.on.ca

Published with assistance from the Ontario Ministry of Culture, Tourism and Recreation

Cover: *Portrait of Sa Ga Yeath Qua Pieth Tow (Christianized Brant), 1710.* Oil on canvas, John Verelst/National Archives of Canada/C-092419
[no relation to Joseph Brant]

Contents

Preface

Today, without a doubt, there is a widespread interest in genealogy in general, and Native (First Nations, Indian, Aboriginal) genealogy in particular. It is also evident, however, that there are few books, pamphlets or articles available about Native North American genealogy (the Cherokee in the United States are a notable exception because they intermarried extensively with whites, and are quite well-documented in historical and genealogical publications).

People of Ontario Native ancestry, for example, who wish to document the lives of their forebears will find that many of the useful records and sources are the same records and resources that are used for the study of Euro-Canadian ancestors (for example, the 1851 Census of Ontario). Restricting one's research to these materials alone, however, would mean ignoring a vast array of other data that are unique to the study of Native people (for example, band lists). No genealogical researcher worth his or her salt would ignore or avoid crucial information; the trouble is, most don't know where to find the key to unlock the treasure chest. The purpose of this work is to offer that key, to facilitate what would otherwise be an intimidating, daunting task.

Background

This project developed in tandem with efforts to accurately document the lives of my Six Nations ancestors. My study in this area began in 1975, with the discovery of a diary written by Patrick Campbell, a Scottish visitor to Ontario, in which he described his trip to the Grand River and his impressions of those he encountered along the way. At one point Campbell stayed overnight with a man named John Young, who had served in the American Revolution "as a lieutenant in the Indian department." Mentioning Young's wife, Campbell commented that this was the first time he had ever played cards with a "squaw." To most modern ears, this word elicits a negative, or racist, connotation — but two hundred years ago it simply meant a Native North American woman.

It is one thing to know that a person is an Indian (Aboriginal). Most genealogists, however, would be less than satisfied with such a broad ethnic identification; rather, they would seek to know the name of the woman's tribal group, and learn more details about her family. Fortunately, Campbell did not disappoint. He went on to state that Young's wife was the sister of the Mohawk chief who succeeded their mother's brother, Captain David Hill.

With this crucial piece of information in place, my expectation was that it would be a quite straightforward proposition to document the Hill family in Ontario and New York. Eager anticipation led to frustration, however, when it soon became evident that major hurdles would impede my research on Native ancestors (for example, the necessity to sift through the unindexed collection of Indian Affairs Papers at the National Archives). Ultimately, with persistence, I was able to trace my Native ancestors in this branch of my family to the mid-1600s, identifying White surnames (e.g., Hill, Green), Native names (e.g., Oseraghete), nation (Mohawk), band (Lower Mohawk) and clan (Bear).

I then determined that I would need to break new ground and set about to ferret out whatever materials would facilitate the task. I shared the fruits of these Native genealogical inquiries in 1981 in the form of an article in *Families*, the quarterly journal of the Ontario Genealogical Society.[1] In the subsequent twenty years, many new discoveries have come to light. It seemed, therefore, that the time had come to update and expand the *Families* article.

Completion of this project hinged on the cooperation of many individuals. My thanks go to Sheila Staats and Tom Hill of the Woodland Cultural Centre, in Brantford, Ontario, for their help and encouragement. In addition, I wish to acknowledge my appreciation of the many lively discussions about Native genealogy I shared with Barbara Sivertsen — they helped to spur me on to new discoveries and stimulated broader thinking on the subject. I wish to acknowledge as well the important contribution of Clifford Collier, Coordinator of the Publishing Division of the Ontario Genealogical Society, for his initiative in convincing me that this project would indeed be a worthwhile pursuit. I thank him for his patience (along with Brian Gilchrist and Kathie Orr in that same regard) in the face of delays occasioned by my move to California from Hagersville, Ontario. Furthermore, I wish to offer my gratitude to Ruth Chernia, who took up the editing responsibilities from Mr. Collier, offered many helpful suggestions and ensured that the momentum kept moving forward to a timely completion of this project.

I would also like to acknowledge the support I received from my former employer, Mohawk College, Hamilton, Ontario, as well as the support I continue to receive from my present employer, East Angeles College, Monterey Park, California. Thanks also to Vicky Nesia, who took a chaotic manuscript and converted it into a document worthy to submit for publication.

This book is designed to be a comprehensive, step-by-step research guide. The purpose is to offer suggestions as to the most efficient way to proceed; to list and critically evaluate each data source (including detailed examples to illustrate major points); and to present a list of the major repositories where researchers can access the materials discussed in the text.

Dr. David K. Faux
Seal Beach, California

List of Abbreviations

AO	Archives of Ontario
AUC	Archives of The United Church of Canada
BCB	Brant County Branch of the Ontario Genealogical Society
BMD	Birth, marriage and death records
LDS	Church of Jesus Christ of Latter Day Saints (Mormons)
NA	National Archives of Canada
RG 10	Indian Affairs Papers, NA
RGO	Registrar General of Ontario
WCC	Woodland Cultural Centre, Brantford, Ontario

Introduction

Target Audience for This Work

This publication was prepared with the needs and interests of a diverse readership in mind. I've anticipated that readers could likely be grouped into one of the following six categories:

1. Persons residing in the general North American community who know or suspect that they have a Six Nations Indian ancestor and who are interested in documenting this link, as well as learning more details about their Native heritage.
2. Status members of the Six Nations (originating in present-day Brant and Haldimand counties) who are interested in documenting their specific ancestry, from the present back to their distant progenitors who lived in what is now New York State.
3. Persons who are aware of their Native heritage (aware, for example, that a grandparent was a Six Nations member) who believe that they are entitled to enrollment as a member of this band and who wish to avail themselves of the rights and benefits accorded to Canadian Indians. These individuals may be looking for guidance in accessing the records required by the Government of Canada to prove their ancestry and subsequently obtain a "status card."
4. Genealogists, of whatever background, who are interested in expanding their knowledge of relevant records and resources available to researchers in Ontario. Ontario is a cultural mosaic. Those who would profess to be knowledgeable in the widest sense will therefore want to become familiar with relevant materials pertaining to all the people of the province, including, for example, Franco-Ontarians, Natives and so on.

5. Historians, biographers, anthropologists and archeologists who could make use of a comprehensive guide to relevant data sources.
6. Researchers who wish to have a prototype or model for use in preparing their own studies of Native peoples who are not specifically noted in this work. This list would include individuals who wish to conduct a genealogical study of their own Native Ontario ancestors (e.g., those who lived at the Rama Reserve on Lake Couchiching) or of an entire community (e.g., the Muncey Reserve).

Focus of This Work

This book will focus on the information that is available to research Natives who came to the Grand River region of Ontario after the American Revolution (post 1783), and who were members of one of the Six Iroquois nations (or tribes) — Mohawk, Oneida, Onondaga, Cayuga, Seneca and Tuscarora — or those who accompanied the Six Nations to Canada (Delaware, Nanticoke and Tutelo).

I have used the terms "Native," "First Nations," "Aboriginal" and "Indian" interchangeably, since all are in current usage (though "Indian" is clearly on the way out). "Tribe" and "nation" are likewise often used interchangeably; the distinction is that the former is typically used in the United States, the latter in Canada.

Finally, for clarity's sake, the approach used in this document assumes that the reader is interested in documenting, or is actually attempting to document, his or her own personal genealogy.

Examples to Guide the Way

It is my contention that one of the best ways to educate is through the use of examples of real-life situations. Therefore, at various points throughout the text, I have chosen selected examples to demonstrate the variety of approaches and data resources that readers can use in their own work. These examples are set apart from the rest of the text by rules.

References and Sources

The books, articles, manuscript materials and other relevant items mentioned throughout the text are presented in abbreviated form.

The abbreviations are detailed in full both in the notes and in the List of Abbreviations on page ix.

Similarly, the repositories where these and other items can be found are referred to both within the body of the text and in the Appendix on page 89. Upon first mention in the text, a repository's full name is given, along with its abbreviation. On subsequent occurrences, only the abbreviation is used (exceptions are made when use of the full name better suits the purpose).

An Overview of the Challenge

Burnham, Fradenburgh and Kerby are not names that immediately connote images of shrill war whoops and beaded moccasins.* The fact remains, however, that ancestors of some people with these obviously European surnames were sons and daughters of the primeval forest — Native North American Indians. Here is a small sampling of surnames associated with individuals whose ancestry includes White and Indian progenitors from the Grand River Valley and surroundings: Anger, Burnham, Dawson, Dennis, Dochstader, Evans, Farr, Fradenburgh, Harrison, Huff, Kennedy, Kerby, Kerr, King, Lafferty, Mason, McKee, Morey, Nelles, Shafer, Stewart, Summerhayes, Vasbinder and Young.

Permanent settlement of the Grand River Valley began in 1783 with the post–American Revolution exodus of Delaware and Six Nations people and their Euro-American friends and relatives in Butler's Rangers and the Indian Department. The Indians and the White frontiersmen of Palatine-German stock who lived nearby were closely allied in sentiments and habits at that time, and the intermarriage between the two peoples that had begun before the war continued in the new environment. Before the close of the century, Lt. John Young had led the way by marrying a Mohawk woman. Close on his heels was Captain John Dochstader, who married a Cayuga and, after her death, an Onondaga woman, while his nephew, Sgt. John Dochstader, married a Delaware woman, as did Private John Huff.

Other than the close alignment between the two peoples in cogni-

---

* Chapter One is adapted from my article that first appeared as "Documenting Six Nations Indian Ancestry," *Families*, Vol. 20, No. 1 (1981), pp. 31–42.

tive and behavioural patterns, there was at that time an economic advantage to marrying an Indian woman. This union would entitle the husband to a prodigious piece of property. These "Brant Leases" to tracts of land as large as nine square miles were to endure for 999 years for the token rent of one peppercorn.

Over the succeeding years White settlers flocked to the Indian lands, pressing in on the scattered Indian settlements. Thus the number of contacts between the two peoples increased and the number of intermarriages went up correspondingly — including the number of Indian males who married White women.

In the late 1840s the Reserve was consolidated to Tuscarora and parts of Oneida and Onondaga townships. Still there remained a flow of population and an exchange of genetic material between the Indian and White populations. The liaisons between them were so extensive by the end of the 1800s that there was then not a single "full-blooded" Indian to be found on the Reserve. Similarly, the even more extensive group of mixed-blood people who remained outside the Reserve boundaries spread their Indian heritage throughout southern Ontario and adjacent areas of the United States.

A large segment of this group lived as Whites and were regarded as such by their neighbours. Two to four generations down the line their descendants have lost all or most of the physical characteristics that would have linked them with their distant Indian forebears (assuming that the mixed-blood person married a White in each generation). The tenuous connection with Native ancestry would be further loosened over the years, as few Canadians then, as now, could name even one great-grandparent, let alone provide details of his or her ethnic heritage. Perhaps only a vestige would remain in a vague but persistent family tradition pertaining to "Indian blood."

The only way that anyone is going to be relatively certain about his or her true ancestry is by employing genealogical techniques to trace upstream and find the suspected Native North American ancestor. Not only is it reasonably painless to arrive at this step, but also, if time, energy, finances and luck prevail, a person with Indian ancestry can often document specific details about Indian ancestors. Imagine not only being able to determine his or her White name, but also the Indian name, tribal and clan affiliation and ancestral village.

The following overview serves as a framework for the details provided in the rest of the book. I am concerned mainly with the years previous to the twentieth century and with those who settled in the Grand River Valley after 1784 — the Six Nations (Mohawk, Oneida or Aughquaga, Onondaga, Cayuga, Seneca and Tuscarora) and the Delawares, plus the Mississaugas of New Credit.

1890–1980 Documentation

Unfortunately, if family sources don't pan out, some complications may arise when researching in this time frame. Much of the data for this period that is in government hands is treated as confidential by the Indian Office in Brantford.[2] Obtaining permission to view their records involves a complicated and time-consuming brush with what red tape is all about and it will, most likely, not be granted. Most of the earlier records that were generated by the Six Nations Superintendency in Brantford have been (mercifully) removed to the National Archives of Canada (NA). Some of the more recent pay lists are at the NA in the RG 10 Series. The staff at the Archives are cooperative in responding to requests from serious genealogical researchers. There is even a separate reference desk for genealogical researchers.

Before beginning research in earnest, the researcher should send for *Records Relating to Indian Affairs Public Records Division General Inventory Series, RG 10* (1975),[3] which is available in a pamphlet from the NA. It lists their holdings of material received from a host of government agencies. (Unfortunately, this document is quite out-of-date, being current only to 1981.) See also notes 47, 48 and 49.

Some more recent biographical and genealogical data can be found in *The Trail of the Iroquois Indians*,[4] and in the files of the Museum of the Woodland Cultural Centre.[5]

1850–1889 Documentation

There is a motherlode of freely available data pertaining to the latter part of the nineteenth century. The Ontario censuses for 1851, 1861, 1871 and 1881 include Tuscarora, Oneida and Onondaga townships. In 1851, the census takers for Tuscarora Township took "place of birth" to refer to specific locality. Thus, instead of just "Upper Canada," the name of the township or closest village (Tuscarora, Indiana, York, Brantford, Onondaga, etc.) is given. Many of the so-called "pagan" Indians are listed by their Indian names in the early census years (unlike the Christian Mohawks, who generally no longer used Indian names). Therefore the researcher should start with 1881, working backwards to 1851. By viewing the agricultural census for the township, families can be located in later years under their White names, and (if they did not move over the years) by using ages and other facts one can link White to Indian names from previous census years. In 1871 the census taker was ambitious enough to provide tribal affiliation under the "Origin" heading. The proofreader crossed out the tribal names (e.g., Cayuga) and inserted "Indian," but this does not alter the legibility significantly.

The band lists and pay lists for the years 1856 to 1888 are available from the NA on microfilm.[6] Thus all the *registered* Lower Cayugas, for example, are listed by either their Indian or White names. Special permission is required to view these records.[7]

Six Nations census records for 1856[8] and 1864[9] are at the NA and have been (or soon will be) put on microfilm and thus available through interlibrary loan. Photocopies of pages of interest to researchers will be made by the NA for a nominal fee. Again, some individuals are listed by their Indian names, others by their White names.

There are assorted other sources that can be selected for viewing from the inventory to the RG 10 Series. For example, early maps of Brant County show occupants (if any) on each lot and concession.[10]

The *History of Brant County*[11] contains a number of valuable biographies. There is also a wealth of genealogical data in the abstracted Band Council Minutes of 1860–1921.[12] It is rather unfortunate that these records also expose a great many details of a personal nature to public scrutiny. There are many other books that, while helpful, are too numerous to list here. Most large libraries have these volumes, and reference to card catalogues under "Six Nations," "Iroquois" or the tribal name should bring these to light.

If perchance ancestors were Cayugas, then the Cayuga Claims Records will be of certain interest.[13]

Church records are a high priority item and the Anglican records of St. Johns[14] and the Mohawk Chapel,[15] along with the Methodist records of New Credit,[16] the Methodist Baptismal Register[17] and the Marriage Registers for Haldimand and Brant counties[18a] should be studied.

132 530 j

Census Return of Indians Under the Superintendence of David Thorburn Esq made on the Twenty-third day of February 1856. (- belonging to the Six Nations)

Upper Mohawks.	Adults 21 upwards		Youths 14 to 21		Children 1 to 14		Total
	M.	F.	M.	F.	M.	F.	
William John.	1	1	1	1	2	1	7
Mary Porlis		1					1
Joseph Carpenter	1	1				1	3
Magdalene Adams.		2	2		1		5
Margaret George.		1					1
David Hill Farmer	1	1					2
Joseph Lewis.	1						1
Abraham Carpenter	3	2				1	6
Magdalene Carpenter		3	2	1	1	2	9
James Porlis.	1	1		1		1	4
Joseph Hill Weaver	1	1			2	3	7
Elizabeth Thomas.		1		1	1	1	4
David Hill Jacket.	1	1	1		1	2	6
John Froman Smur.	3	2	1	1		1	8
Watyathiyostha –		1				1	2
Henry Staats.	2	1	3		3		9
Joseph Fraizer	2	1					3
Sarah Smith.	1	1	1				3
John Hill Jahendarisen	1	1	2	1	1	2	8
David Carpenter	1	1		1	2	2	7
Peter Hess.	1	1			1		3
Catharine Loch		1			1		2
John Herron.	1	1	1	1	1		5
Samuel Coffey.	1	1			2		4
Esther Davies.		1					1
Ellen Babtest.		3			1		4
Nicholas Green.	1	1	1	3	1		7
Kawakensot.		1				3	4
Henry Lickers	1	1			1	1	4
William Hill Jacket.	1	1			2	2	6
Carried forward –	26	36	15	13	24	22	136

Census Return of Indians under the Superintendence of David Thorburn Esq made on the Twenty-third day of February 1856 (- belonging to the Six Nations). National Archives of Canada/C-149399

1785–1849 Documentation

There is no lack of records pertaining to Six Nations people in the post–American Revolutionary era, especially so if he or she happened to be a sachem, war chief or clan matron. The church records described in the previous section are also useful for this era. There are scattered items of interest at the Archives of Ontario (AO), especially the deed of surrender from the Fort Hunter Mohawks.[18b]

The RG 10 Series is again indispensable. Recorded here are the various documents pertaining to the Indian occupation and surrenders in the Grand River Valley. As parcels of Indian land were leased out and later surrendered, a prodigious amount of paperwork was generated, much of it containing genealogical data. The chiefs and others put their names to a veritable mountain of deeds. The book *Valley of the Six Nations*[19] contains transcripts of many of the important documents, plus lists of those who served in the War of 1812.

Other items of particular interest from the RG 10 Series are the property census for 1843 and the census for presents 1847–1852,[20] the claims by local merchants against individual Indians between the years 1844 and 1880,[21] and the minutes of the Six Nations councils for the same time period.[22] Also important are the claims to Grand River lands arising out of leases granted in the early years.[23] Three generations of sachems, war chiefs, warriors and clan matrons put their signatures or marks to deeds and leases between the years 1787 and 1844.

The Six Nations people sold their improvements scattered throughout the Grand River Valley to move to the consolidated Reserve through the 1830s to 1850. The records of these transactions, often including the name of the former Indian occupant, the lot and concession numbers and when and to whom he sold it, can be found in the land records relating to the townships involved.[24]

The family papers collections at the National and Ontario Archives of those families that were prominent in the Niagara Peninsula and had dealings with the Six Nations Indians can prove useful. The Nelles[25] and Norton papers[26] are at the AO and the Brant[27] and Claus papers[28] are at the NA. The Thorburn Papers[29] at the AO are another cornucopia of genealogical information for the Six Nations families. David Thorburn was appointed to settle the horrendous problems relating to claims to Indian land and kept detailed diaries of his dealings.

The Draper manuscripts are an important yet seldom-used resource.[30] Lyman Draper interviewed surviving family members of those who served in the American Revolution, and attempted to construct accurate genealogies. The importance of this unique data cannot be overstated.

Two articles in the journal of the Ontario Historical Society are noteworthy, especially if ancestors were in some way connected with the descendants of Joseph Brant.[31]

1775–1784 Documentation

The American Revolution was a highly significant event for the Six Nations. It resulted in the shattering of the ancient Confederacy and in permanent exile from their ancestral homes for many of them.

At this point, records for any but the Mohawks become increasingly scarce. It is recommended that prior to research in the primary sources, the genealogist become well versed in the circumstances relating to the war. Researchers would be well advised to read *The Iroquois in the American Revolution.*[32]

Many of the records that do exist for the Revolutionary War period were generated by the military authorities. For instance, the Haldimand Papers[33] have some references to individual Indians but are more useful in determining the activities of tribal war parties, and where the various tribes were settled at the time. In the Q Series[34] at the NA are the claims for losses of individual Mohawks — excellent source material for determining socio-economic status and degree of acculturation.

1710–1774 Documentation

Despite the early years involved, there are a surprising number of genealogical records relating to Mohawks of the Anglican faith. Some baptismal and marriage registers of interest are those of the Society for the Propagation of the Gospel in Foreign Parts,[35] Rev. Henry Barclay[36] and Rev. John Ogilvie.[37]

In 1710 three Mohawks and one Mohican went to England, where they were wined and dined and entertained by nobility, and had their pictures painted. Should one of these individuals be an ancestor, the paintings alone† will be of unparalleled significance.[38]

In 1737 William Johnson came from Ireland to manage the es-

Return of Receipts granted to Marcus Blair for Indian Improvements.

Names	Acres	£ s d	$	Witnesses
Polly Hopkins	7	52.10.0	210	Chas Bain & Archibald Blair
Long Stink	4	33.15.0	135	Joseph Young & Chas Bain
Wife of Captain Hayner	6	30.0.0	120	Lewis Burwell & Chas Bain
Wichnehotong	4	20.0.0	80	Lewis Burwell & Chas Bain
John Shephard & Peggy Price	5 50	19.0.0	76	Lewis Burwell & Chas Bain
Patrick Lathain	2	15.0.0	60	Chas Bain & Archibald Blair
Patrick Lathain	2½	12.10.0	50	Archibald Blair & Chas Bain
Peggy & Sally Hayner	1 65/100	8.5.0	33	Lewis Burwell & Chas Bain
Abraham Goosey	1½	7.10.0	30	Joseph Young & Chas Bain
Francis Hopkins	1	7.10.0	30	Chas Bain & Archibald Blair
Teahawaeko	1 3/8	7.0.0	28	Chas Bain & Archibald Blair
Captain Tom	1 2/10	6.0.0	24	Lewis Burwell & Chas Bain
Zinega	1	5.0.0	20	Archibald Blair & Chas Bain
Wife & son of Cayuga John	1 3/10	5.2.0	20,2	Chas Bain & Archibald Blair
Long Stink	1	5.0.0	20	Joseph Young & Robert Young
Aquiacong	58/100	2.15.0	11	Lewis Burwell & Chas Bain
Peggy Styers & Wichnehotong	58/100	2.15.0	11	Lewis Burwell & Chas Bain
John Hayner	½	2.10.0	10	Lewis Burwell & Chas Bain
Wyateanosh	½	2.10.0	10	Archibald Blair & Chas Bain
Francis Hopkins	½	2.10.0	10	Joseph Young & Chas Bain
Caestyash	½	2.10.0	10	Chas Bain & Archibald Blair
Caka androng	½	2.10.0	10	Lewis Burwell & Chas Bain
Peggy Hayner	½	2.10.0	10	Lewis Burwell & Chas Bain
Wichnehotong	½	2.10.0	10	Lewis Burwell & Chas Bain
Sally Hayner	¾	2.0.0	8	Chas Bain & Archibald Blair
Keafseuqua	4/10	2.0.0	8	Lewis Burwell & Chas Bain
John Hayner	39/130	1.10.0	6	Lewis Burwell & Chas Bain
Chucklehead	24/160	.15.0	3	Lewis Burwell & Chas Bain
Hank Shephead	10/20	10.0	2	Lewis Burwell & Chas Bain
	46 44/100	263.17.0	1055.2	

Return of Receipts granted to Marcus Blair for Indian Improvements.
Archives of Ontario/RG1, A-I-7, Box 7 #9

Total amount paid as per receipts on all the lots 803, 33, 34, 35, 36 = | 1055 . 2 . 0
viz - on lot 33 ____ $. 182 . 2
on lot 34 ____ 518
on lot 35 ____ 217
on lot 36 ____ 38
1055 . 2

Incidental expenses - viz
Paid to Cap.ᵗⁿ Torm - for Interpreting &c for upwards of three weeks ___ | 20
Paid to Patrick Lathaine for Interpreting &c for about six days ___ | 5
Paid to Surveyor for attendance - Measurements &c ___ | 24
Two journeys to York and returning - Hotel expences whilst there ___ | 15
Travelling expenses to Grand River and there - taking down bags of dollars | 12 . 4
Two months boarding at Mr Joseph Young's - for self and Brother ___ | 24
Paid for tobacco - for presents to Indians ___ | 1
Correspondence | 3 . 6
Log Stable - suited for temporary dwelling - and clearing 3 acres ___ | 66 . 1
Charge for loss of time - and trouble - 20 p.Cᵗ on $ - 1055 | 205 . 2 . 6
1429 . 3

Form of Receipt :

03193

Grand River _____ 1833.

£ ____

Received from Marcus Blair & Hamilton - Gent the sum of ____ pounds
____ Shillings - lawful currency of the Province of Upper Canada - being the full consid-
= eration for ____ acres of flats at the rate of ____ for each acre. - The said flats lying
immediately below the houses now occupied by Indians commonly designed Shephead
and Captain Torm - and being situate in lot ____ North of Talbot Road in the
rear of the Town Plot of Cayuga on the West bank of the Grand River - The said flats being
my undoubted and undisputed property to sell or transfer - and I hereby consent
that the same shall be purchased from the Government.
Witnesses to the signature
and Receipt - ____

}   { his
                       X
                     { mark }

The lots referred to, are the whole lots of 36 and 35
and the broken fronts of 34 and 33 - North of Talbot
Road - on the North side of the Town Plot of Cayuga
on the West bank of the Grand river - comprising 275 acres.

Return of Receipts (*Concluded*)

tates of his uncle. By the time of his death in 1774 this man had tremendous influence among the Six Nations. He kept copious records, and many Mohawk descendants and others can be followed through Sir William's ledgers and letters.[39] Note especially the lists by village and clan of those Six Nations Indians who served with Johnson in the capture of Montreal in 1760.[40]

Eventually the ardent researcher will want to identify his or her ancestor's clan (always inherited through the maternal family). This can best be done by comparing the Indian name unearthed with those included in the Seth Newhouse manuscript[41] in which the lists of women's and warriors' Indian names associated with the fifty Six Nations chiefly families are arranged according to clan affiliation.

Six Nations Indians, especially in the early years, seldom left written records. White government officials, missionaries and traders bountifully filled the gap. In many cases there is more opportunity for success in doing genealogy of Six Nations families than there is for their contemporary White neighbours.

All ancestor-hunters have experienced the deep satisfaction and emotional turmoil to be found in accurately delineating their family tree. There is a special kind of challenge and reward in rooting out a Native North American Indian in the ancestral background, proving relationship and successfully determining that Captain David Hill, Karonghyontye (Flying Sky), son of Aaron Oseraghete of the Hill and Margaret, was born in 1742, died in 1790 and was a war chief of the Fort Hunter Bear clan Mohawks. The seemingly impossible is only a thin veil removed from reality.

---

† One of the paintings is on the cover of this book. Note that although Sa Ga Yeath Qua Pieth Tow's Christain name was Brant, he is *not* related to Joseph Brant.

CHAPTER TWO

Starting Your Research

Read General Books on Native Ontario and New York

In the midst of doing your genealogical research, in your "spare" time, I recommend that you become familiar with the history of the Aboriginal occupation of Ontario in general (obtain a broad overview) and the history of the Six Nations in particular. The exercise will provide you with hints about where you might head next in the genealogical phase of your research. While the temptation will always be there to push ahead by researching specific data sources (such as band lists), such a move would be very premature. It would be more beneficial for you at this point to understand how the "Peter Green Aughquagas" or the "Clear Sky Onondagas," for example, fit into the picture. Four of the most useful books you can read are *Aboriginal Ontario: Historical Perspectives on the First Nations*[42]; *Handbook of North American Indians: Vol. 15, The Northeast*[43]; *The People of the Longhouse*[44]; and *The Valley of the Six Nations*.[45]

This reading represents a wealth of information for anyone who wishes to understand the historical background of Six Nations peoples. The summary that follows is based in part on information found in these books.

A Brief History of the Six Nations

Archaeological evidence points to the likelihood that the original Five Nations people of what is today upstate New York had been living in their ancestral homelands for thousands of years. Their territory extended from approximately modern-day Schenectady in the east to Buffalo in the west, with hunting territories fanning out from that area.

These Iroquoian-speaking peoples waged destructive wars with each other until, according to some accounts, in the 1400s, Deganawida (The Peacemaker) and Hayenwatha orchestrated the formation of the League of the Five Nations, symbolically represented by the Great Tree of Peace. They became known as the "People of the Longhouse," looked upon by themselves and other nations as a family living in one symbolic Longhouse. The Mohawks were the keepers of the eastern door. The Onondagas were the firekeepers in the centre of the symbolic dwelling. The Senecas were the keepers of the western gate. The two junior partners were the Oneidas and the Cayugas. The Oneidas lived between the Mohawks and Onondagas. The Cayugas lived between the Senecas and Onondagas.

All families in the Longhouse, of whatever nation, were members of a particular maternal clan (usually represented by an animal, for example, Heron). Each nation also had its own set of chiefs, or leaders. Some were hereditary (councillors who attended League meetings); others became leaders based on merit alone (war chiefs and village chiefs).

All of the Five Nations were greatly feared. They warred (generally successfully) with their neighbours, as well as with others as far away as Michigan, North Carolina, northern Quebec and the present-day Maritime provinces of Canada. They displaced and even eliminated many in the process, including the Huron and Neutral peoples, both of whom lived in what is today Ontario; there are still some survivors of the former living near Montreal. Many of the refugees of war were incorporated into the Five Nations.

In 1714 the Tuscaroras, from the area of what is today North Carolina, succumbed to the pressures of White settlement and moved north to reside with their fellow Iroquoian-speaking cousins. The Tuscaroras settled near the Oneidas. From this point forward, the League was known as the Six Nations.

Beginning in 1667 many of the Oneidas, Mohawks and others of the Five Nations were being drawn to the shores of the St. Lawrence River by French Catholic missionaries. A settlement known as Caughnawaga (Kahnawake) was established there; the primary language was Mohawk. Beginning in 1747 another group migrated from Caughnawaga and the Onondaga territory (including Oswegatchie, on the St. Lawrence River) to St. Regis, where New York,

Quebec and Ontario join (St. Regis was also known as Akwesasne, as it still is today).

Two other communities of some consequence were also in existence in the New York area at this time, composed of a variety of refugees from diverse tribes. These communities were Schoharie (composed largely of Mohawks) on Schoharie Creek, and Aughquaga (composed largely of Oneidas) on the Susquehannah River. Other Iroquoian settlements in the area (e.g., at Mount Royal) consolidated by about 1721 at Lake of Two Mountains to become the community of Oka (Kanesatake). One group splintered off from this community in 1881, moving to Gibson (Watha) in the Muskoka region of Ontario.

In general (there were exceptions), the League or Confederacy supported the British in the so-called French and Indian Wars of the 1740s to 1760. This period marked the end of the gradual drift of the Six Nations people toward Quebec. By the mid-1700s the Mohawks who resided in the Mohawk Valley were being hemmed in by their Dutch, English and German neighbours, having alienated most of their vast land holdings. The Six Nations were inevitably drawn into the growing tensions between the American "Patriots" and British "Loyalists." By 1777 the Mohawks, Onondagas, Cayugas and Senecas had largely sided with the British/Loyalist elements, whereas the Oneidas (with the exception of the Aughquagas) and Tuscaroras gravitated toward the Patriot cause.

As a result, by 1783, many of those who supported the British had grown uncomfortable with the thought of living in their former homelands. They then began to migrate to the Grand River area, along with such allies as the Nanticokes and Tutelos, who found themselves in similar straits. There they joined the Delawares, already residing along the river. Some of the Mohawks elected to settle at the Bay of Quinte under the leadership of Captain John Deserontyon.

The Six Nations on the Grand River were governed by their own local councils (hereditary posts until 1924, when an elective system was instituted) and the federal Indian Department (first military, then civil). The upper echelons of government comprised a local superintendent and a hierarchy of individuals (the highest post being Governor General). This complex system represents a blessing for genealogists, because it produced a mountain of documentation to satisfy the needs of overlapping, and often competing, bureaucracies.

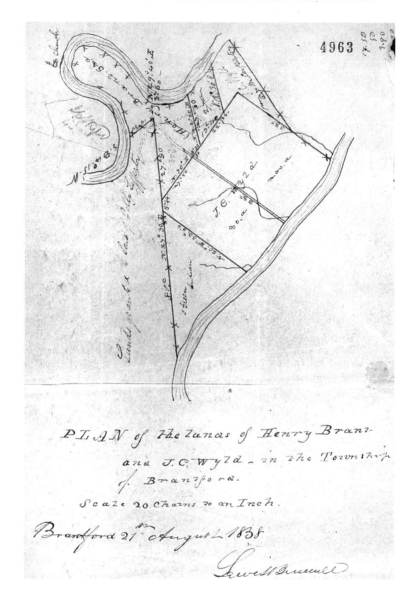

Plan of the Lands of Henry Brant, 21 August 1838.
National Archives of Canada/C-149337

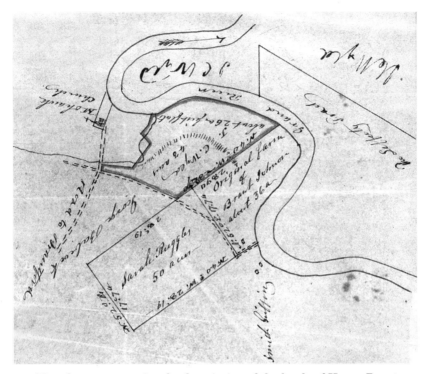

Map that accompanies the description of the lands of Henry Brant.
National Archives of Canada/C-149338

Two main factions soon formed on the Reserve: those who were Christian (Anglican and Methodist missionaries were particularly active) and the Longhouse people, who kept alive the ancient religious and cultural traditions of the Six Nations.

Each of the Six Nations selected geographical territories in the Grand River Valley — technically, six miles on each side of the river, from its mouth to its headwaters. This land had been purchased for them by the British authorities, who bought it from the Mississaugas (who were considered the "owners" of southern Ontario). In general, the Senecas and Delawares lived closest to the mouth of the river, near Dunnville. The Cayugas were split into two groups — one (Lower) near Cayuga, the other (Upper) at Cainsville, near Brantford. The Onondagas and some Senecas resided near Caledonia. The Tuscaroras occupied the area between the Onondaga settlements and Brantford. The Tutelos lived at Tutelo Heights, south of Brantford (with a few living among the Lower Cayugas). The Nanticokes linked up with the Lower Cayugas and Delawares near the town of Cayuga. The Mohawks settled east of Brantford, at the Mohawk Village. There, in 1786, they built the Mohawk Chapel, which still stands. Their settlements spread north to Paris and south to Onondaga Township.

From the very beginning, the Six Nations leased and sold portions of their land to Whites. Captain Joseph Brant held power of attorney to effect these sales until his death, in 1807. This phenomenon, with its consequent influx of Whites, probably explains why some of the nations tended to disperse. Most of the Lower Cayugas, for example, drifted toward Willow Grove (along Highway 6) during the 1830s. Throughout the 1830s and 1840s, blocks of Six Nations lands were sold and the proceeds placed in trust. White settlement of the valley was rapidly swamping them, a growth that was greatly facilitated by construction of the Grand River Navigation Company canals and dams.

The government solution was to sell off most of the Six Nations properties and move all of these people to Tuscarora Township and adjoining parts of Onondaga and Oneida townships. So, between 1847 and 1850, the individual Six Nations members sold their clearings and improvements, and the government removed the White squatters. The Six Nations people moved to their new home, where 100-acre lots were assigned to each family.

Also in 1847, parts of Tuscarora and Oneida townships were sold to the Mississaugas of the Credit River. This area became the foundation of today's New Credit Reserve, near Hagersville.

This very abbreviated background sketch is offered only as a framework for helping the reader to understand the breadth and the complexity of the historical source records that are available.

Aside from Status Indians, How Many Descendants of First Nations People Are There in Canada?

There does not seem to be any accurate way to estimate the number of individuals who are of part-Indian ancestry but who are not registered as Indians. This group would include non-status Indians (i.e., people who have not signed a treaty with Canada or its predecessors), Métis (a term typically used for persons descended from

Portrait of Walter Phelps, son of Hiram Phelps and Maria Smith, b. 1830, one-quarter Mohawk. Cabinet photo, Brant County Museum and Archives (S916). Acc. X977.253

fur traders and Native women in the western provinces) and others having Indian ancestry (that is, someone who has some degree of biological connection to Native peoples; in other words, Aboriginal roots to whatever extent).

The 1991 Canadian census allowed individuals to list more than one ancestral line (not just the father's father) — and more than one million people claimed Native ancestry. Meanwhile, an unknown number of eligible individuals may have failed to claim this identification.[46]

Another factor to consider is the unspecified but sizable number of individuals whose Native ancestors merged into the general population. Through intermarriage, their descendants ultimately "disappeared" into the Canadian community at large. It is likely that, within a very few generations, these families would have "forgotten" their Native heritage (their tribal affiliation, for example, among other details) in much the same way that many Irish-Canadian families are likely to have "forgotten" from which counties in Ireland their forebears emigrated. Many of the common physical traits of Native people (high cheekbones, for example) disappear within a couple of generations, especially if all the subsequent marriages are with persons of non-Indian ancestry.

In addition, for the purposes of your research, be aware that there are many persons of Aboriginal ancestry who have migrated out of Ontario and today are spread around the world.

The upshot is that there may be up to a million people in North America who have a Native ancestral connection to Ontario — many thousands of whom are of Six Nations descent. There are, therefore, many out there who could profit from an awareness of how to trace these links.

Obtain an Overview of the Collections of the National Archives of Canada and the Archives of Ontario

The one repository and record group that is of paramount significance for conducting research in Ontario Native genealogy is the Indian Affairs Papers, known as the "RG 10 Series," at the National Archives of Canada. It is difficult to imagine doing any sort of comprehensive genealogical study without accessing these voluminous and, generally, unindexed records. This collection contains the real gems that entice all genealogists, and a discussion of such items will figure prominently here.

The records are grouped into the following categories:

1. Administrative Records of the Imperial Government, 1677–1864
2. Ministerial Administration Records, 1786–1970
3. Field Office Records, 1809–1971
   a) Superintendency Records, 1809–1970
   b) Agency Records, 1857–1971
4. Indian Land Records, 1680–1956

It is strongly advised that, especially to go beyond the specific references listed in the present publication, the genealogist read one of the inventories to the collection, or published guidebooks.[47, 48, 49]

It is also important to note that many of these records are available on microfilm at the Archives of Ontario. In addition, the AO has other sources useful to the Native genealogist, many of which are discussed in the next chapter. A handy guide to Native-related collections is available as well.[50]

Use Standard Genealogical Research Techniques

The first step in the quest to find Six Nations progenitors is to start with you and work backwards in time. In other words, write down every known fact, especially precise names, dates and places, and work systematically from the known to the unknown. This will entail tapping into family sources — interviewing aged and knowledgeable family members — and using all the obvious genealogical resources pertaining to any resident of this province. One good source is *Genealogy in Ontario: Searching the Records.*[51]

Not only should you check such commonly used resources as the general census records, but keep in mind that there are ore-laden nuggets to be mined in lesser-used resources, such as the Court Records at the AO, and newspaper reports associated with the events that are recorded in them. Robert L. Fraser used these and related resources, for example, to profile the life of George Powlis, who was convicted of murder in 1839.[52]

It is crucial that the researcher know something of the jurisdictional changes to Reserve lands that have occurred over the years. In 1839, the Reserve lands were located in the Gore District. Some reference materials — the above-noted book by Brenda Merriman, for example — include a consideration of this important matter, illustrated with maps.[53] After studying this material you will realize that, by the 1850s, the Reserve was divided between Brant and Haldimand counties. Records relating to both must therefore be explored.

Henry Young, a widower who lived on the Reserve in Oneida Township (Haldimand County), died in January 1862 after a night of drinking with some of his neighbours. A coroner's inquest was held. It concluded that Young came to his end at the hands of Joseph Latham and Solomon Henry Rhodes. It further concluded that Latham's involvement was willful. Latham was ultimately charged with murder.

The inquest brought to light many important details. While the men were travelling home together, it seems that an argument had broken out when Latham accused Young of stealing Betsy Bull's cow, which Young apparently had taken to his brother's place, across the Grand River, on the other side of Caledonia.[54, 55] By referring to the records of St. John's Church, one learns that, in 1857, Young had married Betsy Bull's mother, the widow Ellen Peters (a Delaware). Additionally, the 1861 census of the Reserve (Oneida Township) shows Young, then a widower, and his stepdaughter, Betsy Bull, living in the same home.

Latham was found not guilty of murder later that same year (1862) and, curiously, he married Betsy Bull the next year. Two other Six Nations members were also mentioned in these court records (Margaret Garlow and William Burnham). The moral here: This interesting story was embedded in records that many would fail to check.

Reflect on the Results of Your Research

Part of your work at this point will be to analyze the validity of the information that originally led to your belief that there is a Six Nations connection in your ancestry. You'll want to evaluate where you stand in order to ascertain the next step in your work.

If the evidence available to you at this point includes knowing the person's band number (e.g., in 1932 this particular person was registered on the band list as a Lower Cayuga with that particular number), then you are off to the races. You should proceed to the section of this book that will likely offer the best opportunity to answer further questions you may have about your ancestors.

If you have a strong family tradition about "Indian blood" in a particular branch of your family and your research to this point has verified that your ancestor did at one time live on or near the Six Nations Reserve, but your search of standard sources has failed to provide even the slightest tangible indication of Indian ancestry, you will then need to delve into specialized records relating to the Six Nations. But you will also need to be aware of the need for tolerance of frustration, and you will require persistence to continue looking — even when diligent efforts have led to nothing of consequence.

Let's assume that after consulting a variety of standard records and resources, you have determined that your ancestor was James Dochstader, who lived on the Six Nations Reserve in the 1880s. Family sources have always maintained that he "had some Indian in him." You have discovered, however, that he was listed as "White" when his children were baptized in St. Luke's Delaware Church. Further, he was noted in the 1881 census as being of "Canadian" origin, while his wife and children were listed as being of "English" origin — yet all of his neighbours have "Indian" written in this column.

Another interesting bit of information — which may, or may not, be significant — is that, in the 1881 census, also living on the Reserve, in the household of James's brother Henry Dochstader (whose "Origin" column was left blank), was one Albert Anthony, age 42, an Indian (in other records, he is noted as a Delaware). Meanwhile, referring to the 1861 census, neither James nor his mother, Hannah Dochstader, show a checkmark in the "Indians if any" column (they were then residing in the non-Reserve portion of Oneida Township).

It is now beginning to look as if James was a White man who just happened to live on the Reserve at one point in his life (a not unusual situation). Your grandmother, however, was quite adamant that Hannah, James's mother, was Indian. Where do you turn?

First, it is important for you to realize that the above profile is typical for "mixed blood" families, except for those "officially" registered with the government as Six Nations Indians. If you choose to proceed at this point, you will have to pick your way through the records and resources noted in this book, using as much intuition as logic.

In this example, the written confirmation of Hannah's ancestry is found embedded in an obscure location among the Indian Affairs Papers in the National Archives of Canada (NA). Included in the records is a letter dated 19 June 1845 and signed by Hannah Dochstader. In this letter she reported the results of an interview wherein William Cook (the interpreter) and her son asked the "Chiefs of the 6 Nation Indians" about her status in their eyes. The chiefs, apparently, said, "I am still recognized by them as one of their people."[56] Among these papers is another document, dated 18 June 1845 and signed by James Winniett, the Six Nations Superintendent, attesting to the fact that "Hannah Docksteder is included in the Indian Return for Presents annually."[57]

Reference to the Census for Presents of 1849, meanwhile, shows a Hannah Doxtater among the Delawares.[58] [Note that variations in spelling are common during this period.] This latter record alone, however, is insufficient to support your hypothesis; there could well have been two (or more) individuals (e.g., one Native and one non-Native) with the same name living in the same general area.

As a matter of fact, this is precisely the case here. As if things weren't complicated enough, the 1861 Census of Oneida Township records show that Hannah Dochstader, age 68, wife of William Dochstader (neither recorded as an Indian), was living at Mount Healy in the non-Reserve portion of the township. Reference to the census for South Cayuga Township, meanwhile, shows that, living with Wilhelmus Fredenberg and his wife, Sarah, age 59 (not recorded as an Indian but recorded elsewhere as née Dochstader, daughter of Sgt. John Dochstader and his Delaware wife, Catherine), is one Hannah Dochstader, age 54, residing in "Oneida C.W.," an Indian. She is also a candidate for the Hannah Dochstader on the pay list for the Delawares. This leaves us with a problem. What is the previous Hannah's tribal affiliation?

Another RG 10 document is titled "Application of Hannah Doxstader Oneida wife of William Doxstader." It would be very easy to conclude that she was of the Oneida Nation, but it is more likely that the entry refers to her residence — Oneida Township.

The most helpful clue among the records is a document dated 1806, wherein Chief "Joseph Duquanayo or Thasnoghtha," a Seneca, surrendered land to "Sarah Dennis formerly Sarah Anderson a prisoner adopted among the Onondagas, niece to Thakohenghi a Chief of that Tribe." The wording of the petition of William Dockstader (Hannah's husband) indicates that this Sarah was the mother of Hannah. Therefore, Hannah's father may have been an Onondaga Chief — but there are no family ties to the Onondagas, only the Delawares (as noted above). It is therefore more probable (but not certain) that Hannah's father provides the Delaware link.

Sarah Anderson (who was White) married a man with the surname Dennis. The only person of this name found in this time frame is William Dennis — born about 1770 in Sussex County, New Jersey, son of Ezekiel Dennis, a Quaker residing at Point Abino, Ontario — who lived at Mount Healy on the "Anderson Tract." If this line of reasoning is correct, then the combined evidence would suggest that the mother of William Dennis, and grandmother of Hannah Dochstader, was a Delaware woman. This is, however, far from convincing — but all too typical of research in this area.

It is interesting to note that Henry Young (noted earlier as murdered in 1862) was a son of Ellin Dennis, sister to William Dennis; and he, as well as James and Henry Dochstader, moved to the Delaware section of the present-day Six Nations Reserve subsequent to the tribe's removal from their original location on the Grand River, just south of the Anderson tract. It may also be more than coincidence that, in the census records, a member of the Anthony family (Delaware) was living with Henry Young in 1861 and Henry Dochstader in 1881. Perhaps — but only perhaps — Hannah is related to the Anthony family. Confused yet?

Clearly, some persistence was required here to verify the Native tradition. In many cases, the proof is hidden in some document, somewhere. In other cases, there may be no existing written record that states that a particular person had a particular connection with the Six Nations.

If you find that your ancestor never lived anywhere (Bowmanville, for example) with any geographical or other link to Six Nations people, then you may have to go back to square one and be prepared for a major uphill struggle. At this point you will want to be asking some pointed questions about the accuracy of the family tradition that prompted you to look for a Six Nations link in the first place.

Proceed to Explore Records and Resources
Pertinent to Six Nations Genealogy

The records and resources that you will find in the following chapters are presented in a specific order. It is suggested that you research these records step by step, in the order in which they are presented. In other words, before you advance to more esoteric sources — such as merchants' account books, which are likely to provide only a very restricted range and amount of information — it would be wiser and likely more worth your time to determine if perchance there are answers to be found in readily accessible published books and articles.

Decide Whether You Plan to Apply for Legal Status

What Is Legal Status?

Some people of Native ancestry are permitted to claim status as Canadian Indians, but most are not recognized by the Government of Canada as First Nations people. In 1991 (the most recently published census) there were 511,791 registered Indians in Canada (1.9 percent of the total population), 117,152 of whom lived in Ontario.[59]

These are individuals who are officially registered as members of a specified nation or band (e.g., Six Nations, Lower Mohawk) and who are entitled to government benefits and restrictions by virtue of their status.

In the early years, there seems to have been considerable flexibility on the part of both the Indian Department and the Confederacy (or Chief's Council) in their definition of who was or was not a band member. There appears to have been little consistency here — and much of the question seemed to boil down to political considerations (e.g., whether or not a person had an advocate to facilitate the case). In your research, therefore, you can expect to see almost any conceivable possibility.

For example, in 1835, the local superintendent, James Winniett, certified that it was the decision of the Six Nations Council to allow the children of "White men who had married Indian women" to be confirmed in the lands granted to their fathers, but that none of these children should be entitled to "any further advantage from the lands or funds belonging to the Six Nations."[60] Neither this ruling nor the subsequent rulings seem to have played a significant part in determining who was actually admitted to the band lists.[61]

In 1857 "An Act to encourage the gradual civilization of the Indian Tribes in this Province, and to amend the Laws respecting Indians" was passed allowing (encouraging) Natives to "enfranchise" (i.e., buy out their status) — in effect, this meant they agreed to bar themselves and their descendants from registration as Indians. An amendment to that act, passed in 1869, specified that a woman upon marriage became a member of her husband's band. If, however, she married a non-Indian, she would lose her Native rights, and her children would not be registered as Indians.

The Indian Act of 1876 further entrenched a patrilineal system, so that children of a male Indian and a white woman would be registered as Indians. Significant alterations to the Act were passed in 1951, including a codified registry.

In 1985 Bill C-31 further amended the Act to alter perceived discriminatory clauses. The result is that an Indian woman no longer loses her status when she marries a non-Indian man, and a non-Indian woman no longer gains status by marrying an Indian man. As well, persons who had lost their status under previous legislation could re-register and their children were also eligible to register.

Indian bands now have the right to control their own membership. From the amendment year 1985 through 1993, for example, 160,592 individuals applied for registration. Of that number, 83,797 were successful. The criteria used to assess eligibility issues are complicated.[62] It is beyond the scope of the present work to set out all of the various specifications.

How Does One Obtain Legal Status?

If the goal of your research is to prove descent from an ancestor who was legally recognized as an Indian so that you can obtain legal status, then you should begin the application process. You will need to obtain a copy of the application form from the Six Nations Membership Office (consult the Appendix for the address). Form 83-44 (3-93) 7530-21-036-8459, Indian and Northern Affairs Canada, describes current definitions of eligible persons and specifies the required application procedures. In addition, you will want to consult with the Membership Office to seek guidance.

You may have heard that it will be necessary to also apply directly to the Department of Indian and Northern Affairs, but this is no longer the case. As of May 1995, the Six Nations assumed responsibility for ascertaining membership. Once they are satisfied that you have proven your case (with the proper documentation), they will contact the Department for official approval of your application.

If My Great-Grandmother Was an Indian, Can I Get Status?

This is not an easy question to answer. In reality, "it depends." Apparently, having one Native great-grandmother — even if she was fully qualified — is unlikely to result in your obtaining status. The one exception here is if you can prove that you have another Native ancestor, on the other side of the family. As a rule, though, you are unlikely to succeed unless you also have a grandparent who had (or was entitled to) legal status. This is why it is important to maintain communication with the Six Nations Membership Office to ensure that your expectations are realistic.

CHAPTER THREE

Major Ontario Records and Sources

Published Books and Articles

It is conceivable that someone may already have done a good deal of your research for you. Although all secondary sources must be verified eventually, they just might give you a head start at the task.

For example, some published genealogies can be found in *Loyalist Lineages of Canada* (examples include Sero, Lottridge),[63] *Loyalist Families of the Grand River Branch, U.E.L.* (examples include Brant, Hill, Jamieson, Johnson)[64] and *Ontarian Families* (numerous surnames, along with relatives of the Brant family).[65] *The Dictionary of Canadian Biography*[66] includes well-researched biographical sketches of a substantial number of Six Nations people (mostly Mohawks), for example, "King" Hendrick and his brother Nicholas Karaghtadie, Little Abraham, William Johnson, Thomas Davis, Joseph Brant, Mary Brant, Catharine Brant, John Brant, Henry Tekarihogen, Henry Aaron Hill, John Smoke Johnson, George H.M. Johnson, Paulus Sahonwadi, George Martin and George Powlis.

Other sources include *The Trail of the Iroquois Indians*,[67] which features a section entitled "Biographies of Members of Six Nations Tribes' Designated Chiefs," with information on the following families: Anderson, General, Echo Hill, Jacobs, Logan, Thomas, Davis, Green, Hill, Jamieson, Johnson, Martin, Monture, Moses, Smith and Van Every. In the *History of the County of Brant*[68] you will find biographical sketches of the following families: Martin, Miller, Powless‡, Smith, Wedge, Carpenter, Clinch, Davis, Dee, Hill, Jamieson and Johnson.

---

‡ This name is spelled several ways, including Paulus, Powles, Powlis and Powless.

Descendants of Joseph Brant will have an unusual problem to contend with — an overwhelming amount of published (and manuscript) data to explore. Perhaps the most noteworthy of these works is *Joseph Brant: A Man of Two Worlds*,[69] the most comprehensive and accurate study of this famous Mohawk "chief" yet written. Must-read journal articles include two published by the Ontario Historical Society, both of which focus on the descendants of Joseph Brant and include a vast array of surnames (e.g., Powless, Hill, John, Lottridge).[70, 71]

Vital Statistics and Civil Registration

Birth, marriage and death records (BMD) filed with the Registrar General of Ontario (RGO),[72] dating from 1 July 1869, should be one of the first sets of resources you check. This task has been facilitated of late by microfilming of the index and earlier (original) records and deposit of the same in the AO. This information is also available via many of the Family History Centers administered by the Church of Jesus Christ of Latter Day Saints (LDS).

You will need to write to the Registrar, however, and pay the required search fee if the materials that you require date from more recent years. Because the AO and LDS are constantly obtaining new microfilm, it is the best policy to check with them before you begin your research to determine the date of their most recent records.

If you are applying for "status," you will need to obtain a transcript directly from the RGO. It is important to remember, however, that, especially in the earlier years, registration, especially of Native people, was very spotty; many people failed to comply with the requirements.

Other pertinent provincial government initiatives include a central registry of marriages for the Gore District (1842–1855), as well as Haldimand (1858–1869) and Brant (1858–1868) counties. These records are available on microfilm at the AO.[73, 74] The latter two items are particularly important because they list the names of the bride's and groom's parents (and often include the birth surnames of the mothers). The county registers have been published as well, and are widely available at major libraries (e.g., McMaster University).[75]

The Six Nations kept their own variety of civil registration forms as well, in the form of band lists and pay lists. Records available through the Six Nations Membership Office in Ohsweken include data on index cards. Staff members can access this information in minutes. You need to provide nothing more than the full name of the person you are researching and a time frame. The Membership Office will tell you if someone of that name can be found among their records, along with the band name and number, birth dates and death dates. It is even possible to follow entire family groups in the more recent records, as each person's original number (i.e., the number assigned when that person was listed as living with his or her parents) was appended to the new number that was assigned when he or she came of age.

Church Records

The earliest and most abundant church records pertaining to Six Nations people were kept by the Anglican and Methodist denominations.

Anglican Records

Woefully few Anglican Church (Church of England) registers that exist from the years prior to 1827 include entries for Six Nations members. A few entries were made in the registers of St. Mark's Anglican Church, Niagara-on-the-Lake. These have been published by the Ontario Historical Society[76] and can be found in their original form in the Archives of the Diocese of Niagara at McMaster University, Hamilton.

Not including the progeny of White men and Indian women who lived elsewhere than the Reserve, the early St. Mark's entries are as follows:

Baptisms
5 March 1793 — Catherine Sedthill, of a Mohawk Chief
5 July 1801 — David, son of Isaac, a Mohawk Indian
4 May 1804 — Henry Brant Staats (fil. pop., Grand River)
3 March 1811 — William Barent Staats, of John G. and Betsy (Grand River)
27 July 1813 — Catherine, wife of Capt. Norton, a Mohawk Chief

Marriages
27 July 1813 —Mohawk chief, Captain Norton, married Catherine on the same day she was baptized.
21 August 1813 —Jacob Johnson, a Mohawk chief, to his wife, Mary

Burials
1 January 1798 — An Indian child
29 April 1802 — Cut-Nose Johnson, a Mohawk chief
10 August 1804 — An Indian chief
9 January 1805 — An Indian chief (Cut-Nose)

Aside from these few entries, no other Anglican Church records appear to exist for the interval between 1783 and 1827 because there was no minister within the Six Nations communities, despite the fact that the Mohawk Chapel (St. Paul's) was constructed in 1786. In the 1820s the entire picture changes. Mohawk Chapel records commence in 1827. The original registers are housed at Grace Anglican Church in Brantford. Note, however, that there are still gaps for some years, particularly during the 1870s. The registers from 1827 to the 1860s have been transcribed and published by the Brant County Branch (BCB) of the Ontario Genealogical Society,[77] and these are widely available (they can be found at the Brantford Public Library, for example).

The Mohawk Chapel registers record the tribal affiliations of the parties mentioned and, in the earlier years (to about 1838), the specific location of the individuals' residence. By way of examples, at the baptism of Susannah, daughter of Peter and Sarah Hill, both of the Mohawk tribe, on 20 January 1828, their residence was noted as "4 miles east from the Mohawk Church." In 1834, the residence of Peter Pauls (a Mohawk) and his wife Mary (a Tutuli [Tutelo]) was given as "Tutuli Heights."

Burial records are very few and far between. One document has come to light that provides thirteen names from a burial register that was in existence in 1879, when Lyman Draper wrote to Archdeacon Abram Nelles requesting information. Here we find, for example, that Mary Tekarihogea was buried 23 June 1830, and Henry Tekarihogea was buried 18 August 1830. In addition, the record indicates that Oneida Joseph was buried 14 March 1850, aged 100 years. A note by Mr. Nelles confirms that, in his opinion, Oneida Joseph was "a fine old man."[78]

Chiefs and warriors of the Six Nations Indians with government officials and clergy, Brantford, Ontario. Names include Jacob Williams, John Anderson, Chief George M. Johnson, Rev. Isaac Barefoot, Isaac Hall, Chief Smoke Johnson, Henry Clench, Col. J.F. Gilkinson, Revs. A. Elliott, A. Nelles. National Archives of Canada/PA-120181

A seemingly complete set of Church of England baptismal, marriage and burial registers exists for St. John's Tuscarora (Onondaga Township, later moved to Tuscarora Township) from 1829. The original records are housed at the Archives of the Diocese of Huron.[79] They are available as well on microfilm through LDS for the years 1829 to 1866,[80] and in photocopy form covering the years 1867 through 1914 at the Woodland Cultural Centre (WCC), Brantford.[81] The baptismal entries include each of the parents' tribes/nations (e.g., Seneca), as do the marriage entries, with the addition of the residence location (e.g., Onondaga Twp.). One example of a burial entry reads: "Daniel Spring a Mohawk Chief aged 104 years 9th Nov. 1849."

A photocopy of the registers of St. Luke's Delaware Anglican Church (1888 to 1914) can be found at the WCC.[82]

Methodist Records

The Methodists have been active in the Reserve community since 1823. The movement began at the home of a Mohawk convert, Thomas Davis, and was headquartered at his home in Davisville, on Hardy Road, west of Brantford. Later (about 1830), Methodist quarters moved to Salt Springs in Onondaga Township, where the present church is located (burials here date back to 1822). Unfortunately, few records from this era seem to exist.

The other large Methodist mission was the New Credit Mission, which, from 1847, in addition to the Mississaugas (formerly from the Credit River area), also served the Six Nations community in that area (near Hagersville).[83] The New Credit Marriage Register is available at the AO,[84] and the general registers are housed at the Archives of The United Church of Canada (AUC) in Toronto. While most of these baptismal entries relate to the Mississaugas, a few baptisms were recorded for Mohawks.

One particularly helpful document is the list of Upper Mohawk members in 1826, included among the AUC records in Toronto. Here is recorded the person's Mohawk name, English name and his or her "Tribe" (clan, to be more precise). For example, "Tehonwawenkaragwen Thomas Davis wolf" and his wife, "Sakagohe Hester Davis wolf," are among the thirty-three Mohawks found on this list.[85] (As an aside, this is one example of an exception to the "rule" of clan exogamy, that members of the same clan must not marry.)

In addition, you will want to check records at the AUC of the Wesleyan Methodist resident and "saddleback" preachers for Tuscarora, Oneida and Onondaga townships for the years 1834 to 1874.[86]

Many other churches exist on the Reserve, mostly of Protestant denominations, but their records (generally dating from the latter nineteenth century) are typically in the custody of each particular church or its central repository.

Upper Cayuga Longhouse Records

Other religious establishments on the Reserve include four Longhouses (Upper Cayuga: Sour Springs, Onondaga, Seneca and Lower Cayuga), whose members (formerly referred to as "pagans" by non-members) adhere to the teachings of the prophet Handsome Lake and the ancient traditions of the Six Nations people. Their records, if in existence, are apparently not available to outsiders. While burials have taken place in the grounds around each Longhouse since the mid-1800s (and their predecessors in other locations in the Grand River Valley, dating from 1783), the markers have tended to be wooden; they have, therefore, generally not survived.

Tombstone Inscriptions

Angela Files has provided an important service by transcribing all the tombstone inscriptions from the thirty-seven known cemeteries on the Six Nations Reserve. Her transcripts have been published by the BCB,[87] and are available at many local libraries and museums (e.g., the Eva Brook Donly Museum in Simcoe). Transcriptions exist for all the tombstones standing in the churchyard of the Mohawk Chapel. Some of these inscriptions are very informative. For example: "Jacob Johnson born Sandusky U.S. July 16, 1758 died at Grand River C.W. Dec. 1, 1843 aged 85 years. Chief of Mohawk Tribe." Also: "Peter Brant John who died March 3, 1850 aged 24 years & 10 months grandson of the late Capt. Joseph Brant."

The map that has been included with this publication is of particular assistance in locating the cemeteries and the churches on the present-day Reserve.

One general suggestion with regard to using church and tombstone records: First, determine the lot and concession where your ancestor lived (you'll read more on this in the sections on Land

Records and Maps that follow) and his or her religious affiliation (you'll find further information about this in the Census Records section that immediately follows). Then, using the BCB map of churches and cemeteries, you can make some assumptions regarding which church would have been the most likely choice for the ancestor in question.

Census Records

Two classes of census materials exist that relate to the study of Six Nations ancestors. One is the general Ontario census, which has taken place every ten years since 1851. The other censuses are particular to the Six Nations.

General Ontario Censuses

From 1851 to 1901, the censuses of Ontario include the Reserve lands in Tuscarora, Oneida and Onondaga townships.[88] Microfilm copies of these items can be found in the government documents section of most university libraries, as well as in the special collections divisions of large public libraries.

Before venturing forth, researchers should refer to any of a number of general printed resources pertaining to these records (e.g., *Genealogy in Ontario*[89]). For our purposes the discussion here will centre on how these records relate specifically to Six Nations families.

In the personal census, an individual's name may be recorded as an English name (e.g., John Bompary), an Indian name (e.g., Oghradonkwen) or simply as *eksaha* (female child) or *raksaha* (male child). Typically, the Mohawks, for example, were listed only with English names and the Lower Cayugas with Indian names. Ages recorded should be taken with a grain of salt. Religious affiliation includes the usual Christian denominations, with Church of England predominating; those of the Longhouse faith are listed as "pagans" or "no religion." The 1851 census records are uniquely helpful, because the census taker often included a specific place of birth (the township or nearest village, rather than just "Canada West").

In the 1851 Census of Tuscarora, the following were listed as "Pagans," "Indians" and all living in the same household:

Konwaats, born Onondaga, a widow, age 50
Jacob Silversmith, a farmer born at Indiana, age 30 and his wife
Mrs. Silversmith, born Onondaga, age 18
Kanyode, born Tuscarora, age 1 (female)
Akonhsajiha, born Tuscarora, age 8 (male)
Ronerahhere, born Tuscarora, age 5 (male)

The family relationships remain unclear in this typical example, although it would seem to be a reasonable hypothesis that Konwaats may be the mother of Mrs. Silversmith, that Kanyode may be the child of Jacob and Mrs. Silversmith, and that the other two children might be progeny of Jacob and a first wife. The Agricultural Census for the County of Brant indicates that this family was residing on Lot 7, Concession 5 (or possibly 6), on 100 acres.

This latter fact will be useful in confirming the identities of those with Indian names. For example, the 1861 Census of Tuscarora (Lot 6, Concession 6) includes Jacob Silversmith, no age given, of "No Religion," who is living with wife Anny (age 28) — probably the Mrs. Silversmith above — and a number of children, including John Silversmith, age 13 — who is probably the Ronerahhere mentioned in 1851.

It is worth noting that by the time of the 1851 and 1861 censuses there were still many Native people who had not moved to the consolidated Reserve. Therefore, for the sake of thoroughness, you may have to search all the townships between Brantford and Dunnville — and even beyond (e.g., Walpole Township and the townships around Norwich, Ontario).

As noted in Chapter One, the 1871 census is of particular significance because the census taker in Tuscarora Township frequently recorded specific tribal designations under the "Origin" header, rather just "Indian." The proofreader later "corrected" these entries — but the legibility of the original notation was not adversely affected.

Abram Van Every, age 42, born in Ontario, belonging to the Church of England, and designated a farmer, was listed as a member of the Cayuga tribe in the 1871 census. His wife Mary, age 42, was listed as Onondaga. The six children living in the home (all with this surname) were denominated as Cayugas (their apparent father's tribal affiliation). This example highlights the fact that, from about 1869, for "official" purposes, the previous matriarchal tradition was being replaced with a patrilineal system: The tribe/nation was henceforth traced through the father's family.

It is important to note here that there are two "series" of the 1871 census. One does not include the agricultural census (e.g., the version housed at McMaster University). It will be important, therefore, to ensure that you have access to microfilm that includes a listing of the specific lot and concession where your ancestors lived at this time (e.g., the version housed at the Hamilton Public Library).

In the 1901 Census for Tuscarora Township, individuals in Divison 1 are denominated as "Six Nation Indian," while those in Divisions 2 and 3 are designated by nation, for example, "Oneida." Similarly, the 1901 Census for Oneida Township originally denoted individuals as "Indian," but these were later revised to include tribal/nation membership.

A reasonable suggestion here might be to consider starting with the 1881, 1891 or 1901 Censuses — in which most of the names are given as English names — then work backwards to 1851, comparing the names and the vital information (e.g., ages) of persons living on the same plot of land, ascertained by searching the agricultural census and maps, described on page 45. A more complete example of how this strategy can be put to good use will be presented later.

One potentially helpful book will be *Indians from New York in Ontario and Quebec, Canada: A Genealogy Reference*,[90] which includes transcripts of both the 1851 and 1881 censuses. Unfortunately, this reference also features some errors and omissions.

Six Nations Censuses and Pay Lists

Presents and, later, monies from trust funds and annuities were distributed to eligible members of the Six Nations on a biyearly basis. An early document pertaining to these so-called pay lists (apparently from 1838) can be found among the Indian Affairs Papers at the NA.[91]

The above document's listing of Upper Mohawks includes Number 16, John Green, with three in the family. The payment was received by

"Mary [with her mark] Hill (Daughter)." Remarks include the notation that the monies will be "expended for building purposes." Another states that her father is "intemperate and therefore she spends his money."

Another entry, under the heading "Moses Walkers Mohawks" is Number 1, Moses Walker, with six in the family. The monies were received by his daughter Esther (again, showing her mark). Under the "Remarks" heading you find this statement: "Claimant dead to pay for provisions."

Pay lists, organized by tribal/nation and band unit and covering the years 1856–1888, are housed in the National Archives[92] and are available on microfilm. They can be borrowed from this repository on interlibrary loan. These lists can also be found at the Woodland Cultural Centre in Brantford.

When you consult these lists, be sure to note who signed for the money. If the listee did not, another family member often signed, and their relationship is noted. For example, the Lower Cayuga listing for 1882 shows that monies due to Number 376, John Young, with one in the family, was received by "grandmother Mrs. Curley Sr."

In addition, be sure to inspect the records at the end of each pay period. Some supplemental information is generally included here (e.g., that a named individual was at that time in jail).

In addition to the pay lists, a wide variety of census materials applies specifically to the Six Nations. One of the earliest documents dates back to 1785 (see *Valley of the Six Nations*[93]). This document is only statistical, however: It provides the numbers of individuals belonging to each tribe. The earliest census records were generated by military authorities, and will be discussed under Military Records.

The earliest non-military census located to date is titled "The Return of the Number of the Upper Mohawks." It is dated 31 July 1823, and is housed at the NA.[94] Seventy-four individuals or families are listed. One example is Henry Lickers Junior, accompanied by a listing of two men, one woman and two children in the household.

Another census list, dated 1 December 1835, gives details on the "Mohawk Indians of the Bay of Quinte, who left there last Spring and came and settled on the Grand River." Among the sixteen families mentioned in this document[95] is Peter Claus, a "warrior," and his wife, with seven in the family, including one boy "10–15," one boy "5–9," two boys "1–4" and one girl "10–14" years old.

An 1843 property census, again at the NA,[96] gives details of individual Six Nations agricultural holdings. The list of Tuscarora property, for example, mentions George Mountpleasant, with 16 acres and a house but no barn, two oxen, two cows and three hogs.

By the end of the 1840s, the Reserve had been consolidated in Tuscarora Township and parts of Oneida and Onondaga townships. From this time there is an increasing wealth of census material available. "Returns for Presents" are listed at the NA for the years 1849, 1850, 1852,[97] 1856[98] and 1864.[99] In 1849, for example, among the "Peter Green Aughqwagas" is Number 3, Thomas Funn, with "1 Chief, 1 woman, 1 boy age 5–9 and 1 girl age 5–9." Note that for certain tribes, however (for example, Lower Cayuga), most individuals are listed only by their Indian names, which may present you with additional challenges.

Other census materials exist in conjunction with pay lists and council minutes, dated yearly from 1834 (with some gaps) to the present era. These are kept on microfilm at the Six Nations Records Management Office. Unfortunately, though, they are not available on an open-access basis. The Management Office staff will search portions of these records for you for a fee, providing you can state a legitimate reason for such research. Being a family member of a person on the lists is an acceptable reason, but staff members are empowered to use their discretion when it comes to searching through data. It would be worthwhile for you to explore first the materials that are freely available. Then, if necessary, you can apply to the Records Management Office to request a search of only those documents that might add essential pieces of information.

Land Records

We have already touched upon the types of information that can be gleaned from the various general Ontario agricultural censuses. These are especially useful in ascertaining socio-economic details about the family (for example, the type of farming operation, determined by acreage devoted to particular crops) and in helping to place the family in a particular location.

Meanwhile, there are two other main classes of records related to land that offer important genealogical clues. We can classify these as deeds from the six nations in council and deeds from individual Six Nations members.

Deeds from the Six Nations in Council

The extensive collection of Indian Affairs papers at the NA and elsewhere includes a vast array of leases and deeds. These begin in 1787 and then taper off after 1847. A diverse set of deeds, leases and related documents generated whenever the Six Nations in council alienated portions of their land holdings. The earliest of these records are the so-called Brant Leases, given to prominent White men with "connections" to the Six Nations — for example, those who served with them in the Revolution, those who married Six Nations women or those who were purveyors of goods and services to the people of the Six Nations.

These records are useful for a number of reasons, including the fact that this material provides lists of each chief present in council on the day a deed was signed. On occasion, marginal notations are included, providing such details as the individual signer's tribe (on rare occasions, clan affiliations are given). Sometimes prominent women's names are included. If an individual could sign his or her name, an original signature will appear on this document. But people were just as likely to use a mark.

Quite often, both the Indian and the White names are included.[100] Many of these documents also describe the specific nature of the relationship between the White man and the Six Nations. This information is of particular significance to anyone who is descended from a marriage between a White man and a Six Nations woman.

In separate documents signed at Niagara in July of 1789, the Mohawks who were formerly of Canajoharie (Upper Mohawks)[101] and those formerly of Fort Hunter (Lower Mohawks)[102] deeded their land holdings to Jelles Fonda as a representative of the State of New York. These documents list almost all of the principal Mohawk men and women alive at the time. They include their own signatures, both Indian and White names and, sometimes, clan affiliations.

In the first document, for example, is listed "Sakagoha hester [with her mark]," the Wolf clan symbol (see previous notation re: Hester Davis) and the signature of "Brant Johnson Kaghyakhon," a lieutenant in the Six Nations Indian Department, son of Sir William Johnson and father to four daughters, all of whom married White men.

As another example, in the Fort Hunter document we find "...

young Brant Ago wa nagh tha, kaderin ko wag tea tia tha, agh Si gwari Sere dawett (David)." Other documents confirm that young Brant was the son of Brant Kanagaradunkwa and Christine, and that he inherited his uncle John's Bear clan war chief title of Canadaiga; that "kaderin" was the wife of young Brant and a head woman of the Turtle clan; and that "David" was David Patterson, a Mohawk war chief who died in 1807 and was succeeded by his nephew.

On 25 August 1824 the "Principal Chiefs or Sachems of the Six Nations" confirmed a 999-year lease of 1,200 acres of land to William Kennedy Smith for his two children "by one of our women." The children were named as Abraham Kennedy Smith and "the wife of William Kerby." Each was to receive 600 acres. The chiefs in council signed the said document. Those names ["X" means his mark] include Henry X Tekarihogen, Jacob X Lewis, Aaron X Nicholas, Moses X Nicholas, Daniel X Springer, Henry Brant, Jacob X Brant, William X Palmer, Thomas Davis, Joseph Hess, Wm. Hess, Lawrence X Davids, Henry A. Hill, Jacob X Johnson, Sampson Hess, Isaac X Lock, Joseph X Frasier, Peter X Green, Little Peter X, Oneida Joseph X, David X Frasier, Jacob X, David X Harris, Jacob X Henhawk, Bigroad X Fish and James X Cooley.[103]

In a later petition, dated 14 October 1847, William Kennedy Smith indicates that he "married a woman of the Mohawk tribe by whom he had two children," naming them as Abraham K. Smith and Margaret Kirby, wife of William Kirby.[104] The records of the Mohawk Chapel (as discussed previously) indicate that William Kennedy Smith's Mohawk wife was named Mary Hill, and letters in the Draper manuscripts[105] confirm the names of this woman's brother, Isaac Hill; nephew, David Hill; and a sister, Elizabeth, whose married name was Green. The above-mentioned David, son of Isaac, is the child noted earlier who was baptized at Niagara in 1801.

Deeds from Individual Six Nations Members

The second class of land records we need to mention documents the parcels of land that were sold by Six Nations individuals, events that frequently occurred at the time these individuals moved to the consolidated Reserve.

Many of these records include surveyors' descriptions of the properties in question, as well as some family relationships. With these records it becomes possible to plot the precise location where a Native ancestor originally resided prior to removing to the present-day Reserve. A rich collection of such items can be found scattered throughout the Indian Affairs Papers.[106] If all the information one requires is a bare-bones list of name, lot and concession, it would be helpful to research the surveyors' papers that summarize details of land sales in each township. All pertinent townships are represented in the Indian Affairs collections at the NA,[107] with the exception of Seneca Township, whose land records are in the custody of the Six Nations Records Management Office.

In the extensive collection of papers that relate to the sale by William Crawford during the 1830s and 1840s of his land holdings in the village of Caledonia in Seneca Township, there exists a detailed surveyor's description of the property. These records indicate that Crawford was an Onondaga chief whose property, known as "the Crawford Tract," abutted that of John Buck, alias Clearsky, another Onondaga chief. The parcel was 400 acres in size, and had been occupied by William Crawford for about twenty years. The deed turning the land over to Jacob Turner, a White man, was signed by William X Crawford, John X Crawford, Mary X Crawford and Abraham Crawford (who is noted in the documents as being the son of the said William).[108]

Maps

Cartographic information is available pertaining to the settlements and villages along the Grand River starting from 1779 (the Delaware settlements). These documents are useful in profiling, for example, the location of the Lower Cayuga settlements from 1783 to the removal of 1849.[109]

Even more useful, from a genealogical perspective, are the maps that show land holdings of individual Six Nations members. Unfortunately, these records are scattered in diverse locations. Major collections include those housed at the Office of the Surveyor General of Ontario, in Toronto, and the National Map Collection at the

NA (see their catalogue cards). Some can be found embedded among the land records at the NA (refer to the Land Records section). Still others have been published in one form or another.[110, 111]

Among the land records in the Indian Affairs Papers at the NA you will find a survey map dated 21 September 1836.[112] The surveyor, Lewis Burwell, completed this map to demarcate the property of Margaret Hill's 120-acre plot. It also shows topography; for example, a rise where three house sites are indicated. The Grand River and local roads are shown, as are the property locations of Isaac Lock and Joseph Carpenter, the house and barn sites of George Martin and the house site of William LoFort

The description of the property that accompanies the map (from the Land Records section) includes the information that Margaret is the daughter of Henry Hill, deceased, the niece of Chief John Hill and the granddaughter of Esther Hill and the late Captain David Hill, a chief of the Mohawk Nation. The indenture between Esther Hill and Margaret Hill notes that David Hill was the original occupier of the land, thereby providing continuity back to the late 1700s.

A diagram in the Surveyor General's records shows the extent of the clearings claimed by individual Natives (largely Tuscarora and Onondaga) in Onondaga Township (labelled "Tuscarora").[113] For example, this map shows the irregular clearing of thirty acres owned by Levi Turkey bordering the road and directly opposite the Mission Lot.

Both the Tremaine map of Brant County, 1858, and the atlas of Brant County, 1875, provide the names of the occupants of each lot and concession in Tuscarora Township, as well as the portion of Onondaga Township that was encompassed within the Reserve. For example, in both years, Wm. Jacob was residing on the south half of Lot 1, Concession 5. Meanwhile, in 1858, "Widw Fishcarrier" occupied Lots 47 and 48, River Range. In 1875, J. Williams, J. Hill and L. Johnson were listed in this location.

Council Minutes

Scattered throughout the Indian Affairs Papers at the NA are copies of the minutes of meetings held among the chiefs of the Six Nations, typically with one or more representatives of the government in attendance, for example, the Indian Superintendent. These begin about 1802 (the Claus Papers) and extend through the 1840s, and perhaps beyond (Indian Affairs Papers).

The usefulness of council minutes rests primarily in the fact that individual names are sometimes mentioned. At the very least, the list of chiefs who attended is appended to each set of minutes. Council meetings were held variously at Niagara, at the Onondaga Council House or at the Council House in the Mohawk Village.

On 9 November 1806, a council meeting took place at Onondaga. The minutes include the usual list of chiefs, as well as the original signatures of witnesses Warner Nelles, John Young and John Ryckman. It would also appear that, in this instance, William Claus, the Superintendent, later added marginal notes. For example, opposite the name J. Norton Teyonishokarawen, he wrote: "discharged soldier 65 regt"; of Seth Hill Aghstawenserontha, he appended: "Capt Seth"; regarding John Otonghseronge: "Scotch John Oughquaghga"; Skayendakho: "Bearfoots Son"; and regarding Oghkware Oghsida, he wrote: "Bearfoot Onondaga."[114]

The list of chiefs noted in the minutes of the council held 26 September 1836 at the Mohawk Village divides them into tribe or nation and band groups.[115] The Oneida chiefs in attendance included Oneida Joseph, Peter Green, Jacob Green and Joseph Green.

In general, a relatively complete set of Six Nations council minutes is available. Minutes from 1834 to the present can be found on microfilm at the Six Nations Records Management Office. Note, though, that access is quite restricted; it is permitted only by way of a Band Council resolution.

Again, as in the case of census records, Management Office staff are able to complete a circumscribed search of these records on your behalf. But it can be costly (for more on this, see the Appendix). And be prepared to wait — staff members do have other priorities as mandated by their employers, the Band Council.

Other examples of Council decisions that can provide particularly useful information, but that you can gain access to without the same degree of difficulty, are found in the "Index to the Red Series," with its associated files.[116]

Indian Department officials examined the right of Mrs. John Cayuga to reside on the Six Nations Reserve in 1885. The associated papers in this case indicate that she was the widow of the late John Cayuga, formerly a chief of the Delawares of the Grand River and that she was now married to a White man named James Johnson. Based on this latter marriage, and the fact that "she was a foreign Indian of the Stockbridge Band and so adopted as the wife of a Six Nation," Mrs. Cayuga was instructed to leave the Reserve. The Indian Department supported the decision of the Six Nations Council in this matter.[117]

One reason why the Council minutes are so highly restricted may be because, in the past, some rather personal and sensitive information pertaining to individuals and families has found its way into publication. Some examples in this regard relate to questions of illegitimacy and the apparent importance in the 1800s of assessing the degree of "Negro" (Black) heritage in candidates for a chiefship.

A typical example here would be John Noon's published study of Council minutes for the period from 1860 to 1921. In the main, this is an excellent account. Noon includes very specific information, transcribed directly from the minutes, and the genealogical content is very high. On the other hand, there is something a bit discomfiting in the fact that this material has been made public and is therefore open to rather casual scrutiny.

A relatively tame example occurs in 1917, as the chiefs hear evidence concerning a dispute over disposition of the estate of the late David Jamieson. Material submitted for their consideration includes the fact that Jamieson had first married Susannah Longfish Curley, by whom he had three children, Eunice, Nancy and Wilson. Jamieson then married Lucretia Russel (no issue). Additional information in the case states that, at the time of the submission, Lucretia Jamieson was residing with Melissa Jamieson, a granddaughter of the deceased Mr. Jamieson.[118]

Petitions and Letters Addressed to Canadian Officials

From time to time, Six Nations individuals or groups submitted petitions to the local Indian Department bureaucrat (Superintendent of the Six Nations Reserve) or his "higher ups" in Montreal (the Governor General or the Chief Superintendent). These documents, also housed among the Indian Affairs Papers at the NA, sometimes provide a wealth of detail.

On 30 January 1807 the interpreter at Fort George (Niagara) wrote a letter stating that on that day "Abram Hill a Mohawk Indian from the Grand River" told him that someone stole a mare "belonging to Isaac Hill, Brother to the above Abram."[119] In the package sent to "Mr. St. John" asking for the advice of their local Superintendent, William Claus, is a petition or letter from Jos Kemp, David Patterson, Jacob Johnson, Abram Hill and Dewatohaganega about the incident whereby Isaac Hill's horse was stolen.[120]

On 14 May 1841 Margaret Powles, widow, and Susannah Powles, wife of George Powles, plus a number of chiefs and warriors of the Six Nations, signed a petition to Lord Sydenham indicating that George Powles had been incarcerated in Kingston since May 1839 subsequent to his conviction for the murder of Susannah Doxtader. This record included the statement that George Powles was "the grandson of our late worthy and highly revered Chief, the late Captain Joseph Brant," who "has a wife and child who are now suffering from penury and want."[121]

In the spring of 1843 twenty-eight of the Lower Cayugas who then lived near Indiana on the Grand River signed a petition to the Governor General.[122] What is particularly noteworthy about this document is that all the individuals are listed by their White names, very unusual at this early date. These names are as follows:

George Styers	Young Warner	Henery Young
James Nand Cook	Martan David	John Wiskey
John Schyler	John Warner	John Fish
James David	John Jack	William Silversmith
John Fish Carrier	George Monture	John Smith
Silver Smith	William Curley	John Slinke
John Hodge	Abraham Goosey	John Yonge
John Smoke	John Hill	John Cayuga
Hanis Hiflier	William Fish	James Johnson
John Henery		

Claims for Losses

After the American Revolution and the War of 1812 those of the Six Nations who had incurred losses due to their involvement in these conflicts were entitled to receive compensation. In 1784 individual Mohawks plus a number of Tuscaroras and Aughquagas then resident at Niagara were given a one-time payment based on their submitted list of items destroyed or lost during the American Revolution.[123] A similar payment was authorized for the Mohawks then living as refugees at Lachine in Quebec.[124]

Margareth, Capt Daniels Widow made a claim for £620/17/00 in total, which included seventy-two acres of land at Fort Hunter, a house and barn, blankets, horses, cows, pigs, kettles, a plough and a sled. Other records indicate that Captain Daniel Oghnawera ("The Spring") died 7 September 1775 at Noyan, Quebec. He married Margaret Hill Kayadontyi (sister of Mary) at Fort Hunter 7 June 1750. Daniel was succeeded by Daniel Spring Oghnawera "The War Chief," his nephew, whose burial was noted in a previous example.

In 1788 some eighteen males and ten females formerly residing at Fort Hunter and Canajoharie signed a petition to the New York Legislature wherein they requested the return of their lands, or compensation for same.[125] The two names at the head of the list were Nicholas Onwawennarongengh (Turtle totem), and John Crine Aronghyenghtha (his mark).

In 1817, after the War of 1812 was resolved, it appears that most of the adult Natives of the Six Nations Reserve were entitled to claim for losses, and were paid in three instalments, every ten years to 1837.[126]

Among the Delaware claimants was "Abraham Huff," entitled to £9/12/11 1/4 in 1837, which was received by "John Huff (his mark)." Among the Lower Tutulies was "Curley headed George's son-in-law." J. Martin signed for the monies. In the list of Seneca claimants was "Kaghneghtageh." The funds were received by "William Dickson (his mark)."

If any ancestors were Cayuga, then an essential source is the published transcripts of the Cayuga Claims Commission set up in order to seek compensation for the Cayugas for the sale of their former lands in upstate New York.[127]

In Brantford, on 21 November 1889, Mrs. George Monture was interviewed. She indicated that she was born about 1808, lived at Indiana (on the Grand River) during the War of 1812, and along the Plank Road later, the daughter of the principal Cayuga chief John Jacobs Hay-a-dow-ah, who was born at Cayuga Lake. At age 17 she married her husband, who was over 20 at the time and living in the Cayuga Longhouse with his uncle the chief. He served in the War of 1812, inherited the title of his brother Chief Joseph Monture, and died about eleven years previous to the interview. Their son (unnamed — but Joseph in other sources) died about three years previous, aged between 60 and 70.

Another entry in the above records pertains to Jacob Silversmith, a Cayuga chief for the past forty years, born at Grand River, age about 71. Jacob's Indian name was Te yo to we go. When asked to translate the name he said, "I cannot say exactly in English; it means something like cold, cold weather." His father's name was Silversmith, who at one time held the Cayuga title of Ojagehtti.

There is further information under Census Records and Anthropologists' and Historians' Records on this Jacob Silversmith.

Military Records

There are scattered references to individual Six Nations Indians during the American Revolution in the voluminous collection of records generated by the civil and military establishments. Perhaps the most useful source is the Haldimand Papers, available at McMaster University[128] as a series of 115 microfilm reels of the original papers, including correspondence and lists, held in England.

On 5 November 1780 Capt. Alexander Fraser wrote to Haldimand, informing the latter that among the persons returning from the

Mohawk Country was "a Sister of Captn Aaron the Mohawk Chief, a very intelligent woman who was much in the Confidence of all the principal Indians that adhered to the Rebels, as she was herself always attached to their cause & till now lived among them."[129] In a letter from Daniel Claus to Haldimand dated 30 November 1780, Claus provided further information about "Mary[,] Aarons sister, the Indn Confidante of Gl Schuylers, who having been since this Rebellion begun, a staunch Friend & Advocate for the Rebel cause notwithstanding her being deserted & censured by all her Relations and Friends, at last came off upon Sr. Johns last visit to that Country, and is now at Carleton Island with Joseph's sister Molly."[130] Clearly this information can add immeasurably to the bare bones of a genealogy, and confirms that Captain Aaron (Hill) had a sister named Mary.

One of the most comprehensive documents of interest relating to the War of 1812 is the "Return of the Six Nations Tribesmen at Beaver Dam, 24 June 1813."[131] The tribes represented here include Mohawks, Onondagas, Senecas, Oneidas and Aughquagas, Upper Cayugas, Lower Cayugas, Tuscaroras, Lower and Upper Tutaleys [spelling variation] and Delawares. While most of the Mohawks and Oneidas and Aughquagas have White Christian names and either a Native or a White surname, the other tribal participants are typically noted only with a Native name. For example, at the head of the eighty Mohawks was Henry Dekarihoga. followed by Jacob Lewis Senior. The Oneidas and Aughquagas were led by Oneida Joseph, and the Tuscaroras by White Coat Chief Tyaka we he.

Another list is that of all the chiefs (principal and war) of the Six Nations at the time of the War of 1812. It was composed by Chief George Martin Shononghsese, and is found in the Claus Papers at the NA.[132] For example, the third war chief of the Mohawks was then "John Green Aronghyenghtha" (see Claims for Loss section); the sixth principal chief of the Onondagas was "Ari hon seed corn"; and the first war chief of the Tuscaroras was "Bill Jack Kareahageayate."

Letters typically found among the Indian Affairs Papers at the NA include one sent by John Brant to Col. William Claus on 16 November 1814,[133] wherein Brant noted that on the 6th of November "the widow Hills son Thomas Died of his wounds. Abraham the fiddle killed near Mount Pleasant — Peter John, Doctor Aaron and David Davids severely wounded. Jacob Johnson slightly."

Other documents include lists such as the undated manuscript (probably 1814) in the Norton Papers at the AO[134] listing Mohawks then receiving rations. For example, among the recipients was "David Frazer" with one man, one woman and three children. In addition there are assorted other lists of interest, particularly the list of individuals who had been wounded in the war. For example, on the 13 February 1817 list written by John Norton is "David Davids Karaghkontye. A chief by right gave through curtesy to a younger brother; but through the war he acted ... was wounded through both thighs. about 45."[135]

Family Papers

The personal papers of any family who had commercial or other dealings with the Six Nations would be worth checking. Some of the most valuable are the Claus Papers,[136] the Brant Papers,[137] and the Moses Papers[138] at the NA, and the Norton Papers[139] and the Thorburn Papers[140] at the AO (see finding aids at these repositories to access these materials). Their contents are noted by example elsewhere in this book.

On 7 August 1785 Paulus Sa hon wa dy wrote a letter in Mohawk to Daniel Claus. Paulus provides news of recent events along the Grand River. He also speaks about his distress over the lack of a teacher for the school. He adds, "There are many of the People here want me to take the teaching again. I am prepared to take up the work provided someone assists me with the equipment. And it is deplorable how indifferent the Chiefs appear to be in this matter."

He then adds a very important piece of genealogically relevant information — especially if one is descended from the Powless family. Paulus says, "All my children are well. I have now four children — two boys — and these are their names: Margaret, Paul, Peter and Mary." Reference to the original letter shows that Paulus wrote the names of his children in Mohawk — Konwageri, Paul, Peter, Warigh.[141] Reference to other sources in Ontario and New York demonstrates that Paulus Sahonwadi (d. circa 1788) of the Wolf clan was the son of Paulus Peterson Onihario (d. circa 1780) of the Turtle clan, who was the son of "King" Hendrick Peterson Tyanoga (d. 1755) of the Bear clan, who was in turn the son of Peter, a Mohawk chief, and his wife,

Eunice, a Stockbridge Mahican woman. Genealogists should note, however, that there were two Peter Pauluses and two Paul Pauluses, born within a few years of each other. The father of one set was Paulus Sahonwadi, and of the other, Paulus Shagoyadiyostha, an Upper Mohawk chief. So far it has not proved possible to sort out with certainty which branches lead from each Paulus.

Anthropologists' and Historians' Records

Over the years a procession of anthropologists has come to the Six Nations Reserve to study its peoples, and has left records that are useful to genealogists. For example, in the 1950s Annemarie Shimony explored the conservative traditions then existing on the Reserve among the members of the Longhouse community. She published her findings in the Yale University Publications in Anthropology. This over 300-page manuscript contains unique details about various aspects of Longhouse life, with the names of numerous individuals peppered throughout. In addition, some genealogical charts are used to trace the inheritance of chiefs' titles. For example, on page 106 there is a five-generation chart showing some of the descendants of Esther (Doxstader) General. Recently this hard-to-obtain study has been reprinted,[142] and a nominal index has been included, which greatly facilitates the use of the study.

In the early years of the twentieth century A.A. Goldenweiser spent considerable time collecting information on the Six Nations Reserve. Most is unpublished, and available in original format (and microfiche cards) at the Canadian Museum of Civilization in Hull, Quebec. The unfortunate fact is that Goldenweiser used his own coded script, which is virtually impossible for the uninitiated to follow. If you are related to the Gibson, Smoke, Barn, Echo, Martin, Key or Johnson families it would probably be worthwhile to access these records and wade through them as best you can, since detailed genealogies are included. For example, he includes the Indian names and clan affiliations of the descendants of Jacob Johnson (b. 1758). Another valuable item is the over 500 Mohawk names he collected on the Reserve, some with English translation, clan link and the holder of the name as of about 1912.[143]

Another anthropologist was Horatio Hale, who was active on the Reserve in the 1880s. An entry in his journal, written in July 1883, was described by another anthropologist (William Fenton) in 1950.[144] Fenton described Hale's record of a ceremony taking place inside the Onondaga Longhouse in which the eulogy singer, the "elderly" Cayuga Chief Jacob Silversmith (Teyotherehkonh, "Doubly Cold") entered the building "bearing in his hand a staff, with which he seemed to time his steady walk."

Lewis Henry Morgan came to the Grand River in 1850 on an expedition to collect artifacts. One item he purchased was a conch-shell breastplate, sold to him by Peter FishCarrier Ga-no-sa, age 60, "son of Jo-ja-ga-ta or FishCarrier who formerly resided at Canoga." Morgan also provides copious details about the FishCarrier family, presumably from an interview with the said Peter. Apparently the father of Peter returned to Buffalo, where he died when Peter "was a young man," leaving three children, including Peter, another son (then dead) and a daughter (then dead) — all of whom "have children living on Grand River." Morgan gave very precise information about another informant, John Jacobs Go-to-wa-kuh, a Cayuga, age 74. He was born at the Cayuga Village in New York "three miles south of Spring Port on the deep gully creek."[145]

Anyone interested in the Delawares of the Grand River would be well advised to read *The Celestial Bear Comes Down to Earth*, by the anthropologist Frank Speck.[146] He wrote this detailed work in collaboration with Jesse Moses of the Delawares. It includes a very complete history of the tribe in Canada, and a consideration of the ceremonies still existing among the local Delawares. There are numerous items of genealogical interest, including a careful description of the various chiefs and their relatives (giving White and Indian names) from 1945 back to the early 1800s. A similar study by Speck focuses on the Tutelo and includes photographs and significant historical, anthropological and genealogical data.[147]

Lyman Draper was a historian who visited both the Bay of Quinte Reserve and the Six Nations Reserve in the 1870s. He collected information for his proposed book (never published) on Joseph Brant and on the American frontier by interviewing descendants of Brant and those whose ancestors had served in the American Revolution. His manuscript collection is housed at the Wisconsin State Historical Society in Madison. The series of greatest interest is F, Vols. 13 and 14. An example of an entry is the result of an interview with D' Jacket Hil, age 79, on 26 September 1879. It reads, "Informant's father was Capt. Isaac Hill — (whose father was Isaac Hill also, from Mohawk country) — born in 1762 — died 46 years ago — 1833, above Brantford, aged 71 years."[148] These documents afford unique details, especially for the Brant, John, Green and Hill families. They also illustrate the fact that all information has to be cross-validated with more than one source to seek consistency since informants often gave conflicting information. Note that the informant here, David Jacket Hill, was the child baptized at Niagara in 1801 (see Church Records) and also mentioned in the Land Records section.

Pictures

The Brant County Museum has a large collection of pictures of individual Six Nations Indians (e.g., John Smoke Johnson) and pictures showing clusters of chiefs and others (often named) in the past two centuries. Another good source is the *Archaeological Report of the Minister of Education*, which has photographs of David Key, a daughter of Chief Shorenkowane, Chief John Smoke Johnson, Minor Chief A.G. Smith, Chief Isaac Doxtater, David Vanevery, John Carpenter, Mrs. Reuben, Chief Henry and Mrs. Henry, John Key and J. Ojijatekha Brant-Sero.[149]

Diaries

There exist occasional diaries written by visitors to the Grand River, for example, those written in 1793 by Patrick Campbell,[150] describing members of the Brant and Hill families, and by Mrs. Elizabeth Simcoe from the same era (mentioning Aaron Hill, Jacob Lewis and the children of Mary [née Brant] Johnson).[151]

During the period when the Six Nations were physically moving from their scattered plots along the Grand River to the lands set aside for the present Reserve, David Thorburn kept detailed notes of his investigations of various land claims, writing this information in a set of small diaries. These relate to the years 1845–1862.[152]

Friday, 11 July 1845, "John Young Ind. with other Inds. who had clearings on River lot No 65-3d Con. Onondaga had agreed with

Portrait of Chief John Smoke Johnson. Brant County Museum
and Archives, no acc.

Dennis L. Dennis and their agreement was by me confirmed."[153] Another example is 22 May 1849, when "John Darling from Oneida with two Indians Nanticok and Young Warner came here and made a settlement with Mr. Darling for their improvements on River lot No. 67 Oneida, Peter John Interpreted."[154]

Account Books

It may seem an unlikely place to find a treasure trove of unique genealogically relevant data, but detailed merchants' records of transactions with their Native clients are among the best sources for reconstructing family relationships. Typically the merchant was very familiar with his clients and took pains to be precise, since he had a vested interest in keeping detailed records — to facilitate the collection of his accounts. Therefore these documents tend to be reliable and trustworthy. Some limited early data from the 1790s and the opening years of the nineteenth century are available in the records of the merchants who had dealings with the Six Nations. Examples include the papers of William Nelles.[155] Entries typically refer to members of the Brant and Hill families.

Much more useful to researchers are the later records compiled by local merchants in towns such as Caledonia. They attempted to collect debts amassed by individual Six Nations members by petitioning the Indian Department. Most records pertain to the 1840s through to the 1880s. All are found among the Indian Affairs Papers at the NA.[156]

N. & T. Garland of Caledonia submitted an account on 13 May 1876 wherein they listed Lower Cayuga, Delaware and Oneida debtors, and the dates and amounts of individual debts. The lists are very extensive and seem to include the names of most adults in these nations. For example, on 9 June 1873 Oliver Anthony, a Delaware, ran up a tab for $4. After his name someone wrote "Dead." It appears that Oliver Anthony passed away sometime between 9 June 1873 and 13 May 1876.

Furthermore, at least during the 1850s, many Onondagas tended to frequent the store run by Widow Scobie. Her claims list numerous

The Six Nation Indians to N. & T. Garland, 13 May 1876. A page of the
account book. National Archives of Canada/C-149339

persons noted as Onondagas. Sometimes the information is more detailed than described in the previous example.

On 17 August 1853 William Young, an Onondaga, was produced by the claimants as a witness and swore, "I am the son of the widow Mary Young who died more than a year ago. I am known to my mother getting womans boots & childrens out of McDonalds store at Caledonia. The most was got in the spring of 1850." In the 1851 Census of Tuscarora her name is noted as Ellen.

Computer Resources

While this is a subject beyond the limited aims of the present work, it is clear that at the moment Internet resources are of limited use for those seeking to document Six Nations ancestry. Over time this will likely change dramatically. See *Cyndi's List*[157] for a good selection of online resources available to researchers. However, for the present, the researcher will be faced with the task of accessing the original sources I have noted, so a lot of old-fashioned legwork will be required.

CHAPTER FOUR

Major New York Records and Sources

Eventually the ambitious genealogist will want to see how far back in time and space he or she can travel in profiling a Six Nations ancestral background. Unfortunately the records for all but the Mohawks become more and more sparse as the years roll back across the eighteenth century. For this reason, and because the primary focus of this study is on records and sources pertaining to the Six Nations of the Grand River, Ontario, this chapter will explore only the three major sources relevant to the study of Mohawk families in New York.

Those researching other tribal connections in New York will perhaps be assisted by the efforts of groups such as the Cornplanter's Descendants Association for the Seneca (see Appendix). Ask the knowledgeable staff at the Woodland Cultural Centre for the name of an appropriate contact person.

Church Records

The Mohawks began converting to Christianity in the 1640s, and by the end of the century substantial numbers were at least nominal members of the Dutch Reformed Church and later the Anglican Church. The vast majority of adults had received baptism by the early years of the eighteenth century, and the baptism of infants was virtually universal among this tribe. Relatively few couples, however, married in the church, and burial records are virtually non-existent. Nonetheless, in some cases it will be possible to trace Mohawk ancestors, generation by generation, back to individuals born in the mid-1600s.

The first church to seek out Mohawk converts ("proselytes") was the Dutch Reformed Church. The baptismal entries, including Mohawk converts and their children, appear in the Albany registers between 1690 and 1754. There are over 400 entries dating from this interval. The earlier entries sometimes include the age of the individual, relationships to others being baptized and, in addition to the baptismal name, the Native name and its translation. It is imperative that genealogists search the original records (written in Dutch, and not on microfilm) at the New York State Library in Albany.[158] Despite the fact that the Albany registers were transcribed by the Holland Society of New York and published with an index, that index does not include the Mohawk entries. Even more damaging is the fact that the transcribers omitted about 100 entries. Clearly their agenda was to provide a thorough translation and transcription of the entries pertaining to the Dutch inhabitants of Albany, and other entries were deemed less consequential.

An even worse situation is found with the church at Schenectady. Beginning in 1698 many Mohawk parents brought their children to the Schenectady Reformed Dutch Church for baptism, and continued to do so until 1774 (later entries appear to be Oneidas). In this period about 200 Mohawk children were baptized. These records are also in Dutch (much easier to read than the Albany registers) and are on microfilm and available from LDS.[159] Again, despite the fact that there have been two transcriptions of the records, both are woefully inadequate. The typescript found at the Montgomery County Archives in Fonda, New York, includes only a handful of the Mohawk baptisms. The unwary might conclude that it is a complete transcript and so not check the original records. Even more indefensible is a very recent transcription that included the entries relating to Black slaves but fails to record even one of the over 200 Mohawk entries.

The Anglican Church (Church of England, Society for the Propagation of the Gospel in Foreign Parts) was also active among the Mohawks from early times. One set of documents covers the period from 1712 to 1719, but, with one exception (1712–1713), records only the baptismal names of children — no parents' names.[160] More useful are the records of Rev. Henry Barclay from 1735 to 1746 (he often included the Indian names of the parents as well as the sponsors)[161] and Rev. John Ogilvie, who was minister to the Mohawks between 1750 and 1759 (he seems to have had a marriage blitz, since there are an unprecedented number of Mohawk marriages recorded in his registers).[162]

Unfortunately the registers of Rev. John Stuart, who worked among the Mohawks from 1769 until the exodus of 1777, apparently have not survived, nor have those of Rev. John Jacob Ehl, who ministered to the Mohawks at Canajoharie in the mid-1700s.

The Lutheran and Reformed Dutch Churches at Schoharie also ministered to the local Native population,[163, 164] but there are relatively few entries that can be linked to Natives who ultimately came to Canada. There are, however, a few important entries in the Caughnawaga Reformed Dutch Church registers.[165]

While it may seem like a dismal prospect to read church entries in Dutch, the work has already been done by Barbara Sivertsen, who has transcribed all the relevant entries in the above church registers and has included them, with genealogical charts, in her recently published book. This work is absolutely indispensable for those who wish to link their nineteenth-century ancestors with the generations who lived in the two previous centuries. In essence, Ms. Sivertsen has used all of the sources noted in this section, and has produced a comprehensive, trustworthy and unparalleled study that will save the genealogical researcher much time and effort.[166]

Jelles Fonda Account Books

As in Ontario, merchant account books are a genealogically useful resource. The earliest example is the Evert Wendell Indian Account Book at the New York Historical Society, with entries covering the years 1695 to 1726.[167] The most useful set of such records are two existing account books from Jelles Fonda. One dates from 1752 to 1764,[168] and the other from 1755 to 1777.[169] Fonda owned a store located across the Mohawk River from the Fort Hunter Lower Mohawk village. In some cases, especially in relation to the more prominent families (e.g., Green, Hill, Claus), it is possible to tie most members of a family together and compare the results with the information found in the various New York church registers and sundry Canadian documents.

Sir William Johnson Papers

In 1737 William Johnson arrived in America to tend to his uncle's business interests in this part of the world. He soon became the wealthiest and most powerful man on the New York frontier. His relationships with the Mohawks were unique; he developed close connections with them through liaisons with two or three of their women, each of whom bore him a number of children. What is important here is that he kept voluminous records, most of which have been published in the form of thirteen large volumes.[170] Of significance is the fact that there is a comprehensive index to the entire collection. The records included in this series include account ledgers (including details such as burials of named individuals), lists of Mohawks who participated in a 1760 campaign of the French and Indian War (with village of residence, clan and baptismal and Native names noted) and correspondence that names numerous members of the tribe and frequently includes details about their relatives.

The following example is meant to show how the various records from Ontario and New York can be combined to create a well-documented genealogy and family history.

Family sources provided an original land deed signed by the Six Nations chiefs in council that described Joseph Young as "one of our people." A copy of the deed was also found in the Indian Affairs Papers in the National Archives.[171] The various Loyalist sources indicate that Joseph Young of the Grand River was the youngest son of Lt. John Young of the Six Nations Indian Department. As noted previously, a diary published in 1793 by a Scottish visitor to the Grand River provided the information that the wife of Lt. Young of the Indian Department was the "sister of a chief of the Mohawke nation who succeeded Captain David." Elsewhere the visitor said that in his interview with Captain David's son Aaron Hill, the latter told him that the traditions of the Six Nations were followed and his cousin (father's sister's son) inherited his father's titles.

Subsequent research using the Census of Niagara in 1783 provided the name (Catharine) and birth date (1747) of Joseph's mother. The account books of Jelles Fonda of New York (dated 1755–1777) gave the relationships between the members of the Hill family, as did the records of the Anglican and Reformed Dutch churches of the Mohawk Valley. The 1784 Claims for Losses of Mohawks during the American Revolution confirmed that Catharine's mother, Mary Hill, was the wealthiest woman among the Lower Mohawks. Mary's Indian name was Kateriunigh (1789 Deed of Sale of Mohawks formerly of Fort Hunter), which translates to "She Carries the News" (translation by Reg Henry).

An examination of the contents of a series of land deeds in, for example, the Indian Affairs Papers, showed that David Hill's Indian name was Karonghyontye (translated as "Flying Sky," according to the Claus Papers). These same documents, as well as the engraving on a pistol originally given as a gift to David Hill (in possession of an American collector), confirmed that the Hill family were members of the Bear clan of Mohawks (supported by the inclusion of almost all their Indian names on a list of Mohawk Bear clan names from the nineteenth century), and that Catharine's eldest brother, Seth Hill Kanenkaregowa (his powder horn is in the possession of another American collector), inherited his uncle David's title of "Captain" and the Bear clan sachemship of Astawenserontha.

In a previous example it was shown that Captain Aaron Hill had a sister named Mary. Other contemporary documents indicate that Aaron had a brother David. A record from the Revolutionary War noted that "this evening Lt. John Hill wounded his brother David a Mohawk chief." The Jelles Fonda account book indicates that among his best Mohawk clients were those with the surname Vanderberg (Dutch for "of the hill"), including a David, Aaron and John. Fonda's records state that John Vandebarrack had a brother Aaron, and that David Van De barack [alternative spellings] had a sister Mary. The entries in David's account cross-reference to those in the account of Mary (or Wari, the Mohawk version of the name), wife of Hendrick Sadoquot. Her accounts and those of her husband note that Mary had sons Seth and John (stepsons to Hendrick). Finally, David's accounts mention his mother, Margaret. The Claus Papers confirm that Aaron's uncle was Johannes Crine (John Green), also known as "White Hans," who was the brother of Margaret (both of them were baptized at Schenectady, Margaret in 1712 and Johannes in 1721).

Turning to the various church registers noted above, we find that Aaron Oseraghete (recorded as Aaron of the Hill in the Johnson accounts), baptized at Albany in 1708, and his wife Margaret had children Aaron, John, Peter, Catharine and David baptized at Fort Hunter between 1735 and 1746. They also had a daughter Mary (Maria), whose first marriage was to Johannes (John), son of Seth, in 1747 at Albany, and the daughter "young Margaret," who married Daniel Oghnawera at Fort Hunter in 1750. The church records allow the researcher to proceed back three more generations: Aaron's

Letter written by David Hill in Mohawk, with translation, Niagara, 30 May 1784. National Archives of Canada/M619 Fl. Claus Family Papers, Vol. 4, p. 29. Translation:

Niagara, May 30th 1784

Just another, Brother-in-law, that you will tell what my wife has done, namely she sends her thanks to Sir John Johnson for the clothes (dress) parents were Cornelius Thannewanege and Catharine Karahages; Margaret's were Crine Uniquandihonji and Anna. On Aaron's side, Cornelius's parents were Arie Kanaghowende (whose mother was Maria) and Catharina (whose mother was Sarah). These data bring the line back to births of individuals in the early 1600s.

Researchers should remember that although some lines can be traced back to the 1600s, this is likely to be a rare event — even for those whose ancestors are Mohawks. Most lines will run into a dead end in the early 1800s. This situation is not so very different from those whose ancestors came from Ireland during the Potato Famine of the 1840s, and should not discourage researchers.

---

he gave her. She '*Ga wen ni yo*' Thanks him very very much, and I also thank Sir John for all he has done for us two.

This is all I write

David Hill

*Ka rongh yon tye

* 'Flying Sky.' The elements of the name are as follows: *Ka rongh y-*, from *ga ron gh ya* 'sky, firmament, heavens'; -*on tye*, from the present imperfect tense of an irregular verb, *da ga den*, to fly.

CHAPTER FIVE

Special Research Problems

What follows is a consideration of a number of issues and matters particular to the study of Six Nations families.

Bogus Genealogies

Over the years the author has received many requests for assistance from individuals who want verification of traditions of Indian ancestry in their family. Unfortunately it seems that most are without substance (based just on surname, time frame and geography alone, it should be fairly obvious). It seems that a number of people seem to have a pressing and urgent "need" to find a connection to Native North America. Unfortunately, this attitude breeds a tendency to jump to conclusions and a failure to properly evaluate the evidence (particularly, ignoring evidence that does not fit with their preconceptions). It is the same phenomenon that causes someone to assume a connection with a famous person or the aristocracy based on little more than wishful thinking. This disturbing attitude can cause all sorts of havoc in this area of research.

A number of years ago an individual wrote to me with the information that she was a descendant of Paulus, son of "King Henry," the famed Mohawk chief who died in 1755. Unfortunately, the data in the available documentation clearly make her hypothesis highly suspect. Her ancestor's surname was "Hendrickson" (a name found among the Dutch at Albany). However, there was never an instance in New York (or Ontario) where that name was employed as a surname among the Mohawks. King Henry went by the surname Peters (Peterse, Peterson),

From an Original Drawing in the Possession of James Boswell Esqr.

Joseph Thayendaneken, The Mohawk Chief. Line engraving, National
Archives of Canada/C-100705

Chief John Brant (Ahyouwaeghs) of Joseph Brant. Photolitho, National
Archives of Canada/C-123161

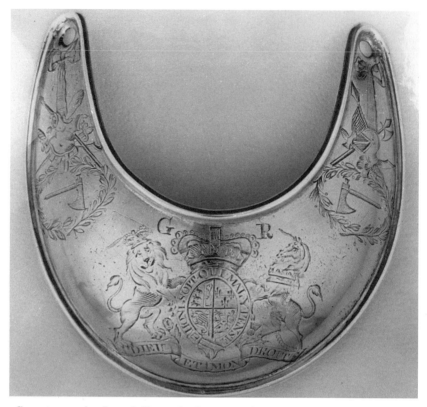

Gorget worn by Joseph Brant in the engraving on page 70. Brant County Museum and Archives

and his son Paulus also only used Peters(on) — his descendants (to this day) used Paulus (now Powless) as their surname. It is very regrettable when individuals make unwarranted assumptions and must be informed (since they asked) that there is no evidence in support of their claim because their claim is likely entirely erroneous.

There seems to be a particular tendency to claim relationship to the most famous of all Six Nations individuals — Captain Joseph Brant Thayendanegea. Frequently the family tradition seems to be that an ancestor was "a sister of Joseph Brant." This claim rests on very shaky ground, because the documents in both New York and Ontario are consistent: Joseph had only one sister, Mary, who married Sir William Johnson. Her descendants are thoroughly documented. Curiously, it has been the author's experience that while the person claiming descent from a sister of Joseph Brant is typically wrong in their specific identification, they *can* frequently be found to have a Six Nations ancestor (albeit not from quite so "famous" a family as the Brants). More troubling are the seriously flawed claims in relation to direct descent from Joseph himself.

Over the years a number of Americans with the surname Brant have tried to forge a connection with Joseph Brant. At the Joseph Brant Museum in Burlington and the Brant County Museum in Brantford are a number of items in the files, plus two books, that all make the same claim. For example, there is a chart submitted by a woman who was the great-granddaughter of one John Henry Brant, supposedly based on material given to her by her father. The chart indicates that John Henry Brant was likely born about 1820 or later (judging by the ages of his children) and died in 1897. He lived in Ligonier, Pennsylvania. The author claims that John Henry Brant and the latter's brother, Abraham Brant, were 15/16 Indian, the sons of Isaac Brant (son of Chief Joseph Brant).

The problem here is that there is no evidence to support this contention. First, it should be noted that Brant was a very common White surname in Pennsylvania at this time. Also, the children of Isaac Brant (son of Joseph) and their descendants are well documented in the journal and book articles noted earlier in this book. Furthermore, Isaac Brant died in 1795, and so could not have fathered John Henry and Abraham. It is difficult to see how any competent genealogist could look at the timing and not see red flags. Even if the person tried to maintain that John Henry Brant's father was Isaac Brant Jr. (see the works noted below), the fact that he died in 1817 is also damaging to the assertion.

The fact is that the records for the descendants of the children and grandchildren of Joseph Brant are detailed and complete. None had any of the children named in the American genealogies and none had any connection with Pennsylvania. A similar item from another member of this family includes a telling note at the bottom of the chart that the compiler tried to use this information based on descent from

Joseph Brant to join the Daughters of the American Revolution, "but had trouble."

Finally, perhaps the most "impressive" studies include a book entitled *The Brant-Overlin Saga*, written in 1953,[172] and a pamphlet entitled *The Brant Family* (copy available at the Brant County Museum). First, the authors propose that Jacob Brant, born about 1770, was the son of Joseph Brant of Ontario, spent considerable time in New Hampshire and at age 21 married an English woman named Mary Lancaster. They resided in New Hampshire during the interval between 1792 and 1798, then moved to New York, settling forty miles south of Albany. Their children were Oliver, Jacob, Sarah, John and Joseph. The author states that Jacob enlisted in the United States Army on 22 September 1814 and served in the War of 1812, but when discharged in December 1814, promptly deserted his family who, in turn, moved to Indiana in 1815.

The genealogy of Jacob Brant, true son of Joseph, is well-documented. First, he was a child of Joseph's third wife, Catherine, whom Joseph married *circa* 1782. Clearly the American Jacob (whose first child was born in 1792) and the Canadian Jacob (born after 1782) cannot be the same man, based on this information alone. Jacob, son of Joseph, did not marry a Mary Lancaster, but Lucy McCoy, by whom he had six children: Jacob, John, Squire, Peter, Christina and Charlotte, all of whom lived on the Six Nations or New Credit reserves. Jacob lived on the New Credit Reserve until his death in 1846.

There is no doubt about the true descendants of either Isaac or Jacob. The claims of these Americans simply cannot be supported. The primary error is assuming that an ancestor who resided in the United States and was named Isaac Brant must be identical to the "famous" Isaac Brant from Canada. What is particularly troubling is that members of this family from time to time travel from as far away as California to Brantford to attend ceremonies in honour of Joseph Brant, and at times have been feted as returning celebrities. This is a most embarrassing situation that is unfortunate for all concerned.

Clans and Native Names

One facet of Six Nations genealogical research that differs dramatically from that pertaining to Euro-Canadian family research is the concept of the clan. All Six Nations people have a clan, which is inherited matrilineally (via the mother's mother). The Mohawks and Oneidas have only three clans: Turtle, Bear and Wolf. The Onondaga, Cayugas and Seneca have not only those three, but also, for example, Heron, Snipe, Eel, Beaver, Deer and Hawk. Individuals were born into the same clan as their mothers. In past times clan exogamy required that persons not marry anyone from the same clan. By the end of the nineteenth century, many persons on the Six Nations Reserve were probably unaware of the clan of their birth. Others, however, particularly those living at the eastern end of the Reserve, still followed the ancient ways, including honouring the importance of the clan in community life.

Recently there appears to be a renewed flourishing of interest in the clan within the Reserve community. The WCC can provide the names of individuals who are now actively involved in the study of this subject.

Ascertaining clan membership, if not known now, can be very tricky, especially since few records provide this information. As noted above, some of the notes taken by anthropologists include informants' and their family members' clans. Those of a chiefly lineage would be more likely to have a fighting chance at discovering an ancestor's clan. There are numerous, but very scattered, compilations of the names of chiefs holding a particular clan title in a particular year. If these persons are not direct ancestors, but members of the extended family, then your search for a clan identification might prove successful. Full brothers and sisters would be of the same clan, their mother's clan. If you know that your ancestor's mother's brother was of the Wolf clan, then you should be safe in assuming that your ancestor was also of the Wolf clan.

Often, by using census or other data sources, you will discover the Indian name of an ancestor. It may not be the name of one of the fifty hereditary chiefs of the Six Nations, but it is still feasible to find the clan simply by knowledge of the warrior's or woman's Native name, thanks to a very important manuscript by Seth Newhouse.[173]

Suppose that you know that the Mohawk Henry Aaron Hill's Indian name was Genwendeshon. Referring to the manuscript created by Seth Newhouse in the late 1800s, we turn to the list of women's and warriors' names under each of the nine chiefly titles (three per clan). On page 246 Newhouse gives the names associated with the Chief

Sharenhowaneh Wolf clan family. One of the twenty-two warriors' names is Ken-wen-des-honh. Therefore, assuming that Newhouse's informant was correct, your ancestor is of this clan and family. Again, a good awareness of phonetics is going to be of immense help, since spelling in those days varied so drastically.

The names themselves appear to have been of at least two types. First there were the family and clan names that were "recycled" back into the pool upon the death of the holder. The clan mother would know the list of her set of family/clan names and, upon the birth of a child, would have assigned the infant one of these names.

It seems that a person did sometimes exchange this name for another, but the reasons why this would happen are obscure. While names tended to be inherited matrilineally, there are documented examples of a son assuming his father's name upon the death of the latter. For example, Johannes Crine was Uniquandihonji, as was his father Crine; Captain Isaac Hill was Anonsoktea, as was his father Isaac; and Peter John Deserontyon took the name of his famous father, Captain John Deserontyon.

Ultimately you will probably want to learn the meaning or translation of the Native name. There are few published resource guides here. Generally you will find a few examples in a variety of different sources.[174] There are some persons who are knowledgeable in the Six Nations languages. Unfortunately one of the most outstanding, Reg Henry, has recently passed away. It might be productive to contact the WCC and inquire if there is anyone they can recommend. There are a number of academics (linguists) who are well versed in one or more of the Six Nations languages; however there does not seem to be a mechanism whereby the general public can contact them to make inquiries about individual Indian names.

Irregular Unions

Even a cursory inspection of the Ontario census records will point clearly to Six Nations family constellations that are less typical than those in the surrounding White communities. Often there are individuals in the same household with a wide variety of surnames and ages. Comparing the listings in the 1871 and 1881 records, for example, shows that the composition of each family unit can shift dramatically, with adults apparently living in a new, common-law type of relationship, and another set of children in the home. Since the Six Nations community contains strong elements of a matrilineal emphasis, the above situation was of little concern. It is imperative that researchers recognize the realities here, and take appropriate caution before making assumptions about biological connections in Six Nations families

There are, however, many family units that were "stable," in the sense that the census data points to the likelihood that the original couple stayed together and the children tended to stay at home with the parents (often in an apparently patrilineally organized household). In other words, as a rule the variability in family structure is higher in Six Nations families relative to that in the Euro-Canadian families living in the surrounding townships. Shimony has commented on the prevalence of "illegitimacy" in the conservative families on the Reserve.[175]

Linking White and Indian Names

One of the major hurdles that you may face is to be able to say whether a person with an English name (e.g., John Buck) in one record is the same individual as a person with a Native name (e.g., Dehowenagriough) in another record. The example below is detailed since it reflects typical hurdles impeding the genealogical study of families who were not particularly prominent in the community, and suggests an approach or method to cope with commonly occurring problems.

We will assume that you know that from family sources (that still need to be verified) that your great grandparents were Robert and Madelina Sawyer, who lived in Hagersville on the edge of the New Credit Reserve (adjoining the Six Nations Reserve). Clearly, from the date of birth of their earliest known child (in 1881, we will say), they must have been married in the late 1870s or very early 1880s. Your goal is to explore the roots of Madelina Sawyer, who, according to your grandmother, was a Six Nations woman who married a member of the New Credit Mississaugas. The Six Nations Membership Office does not have any information on your ancestor, so it will be necessary to turn elsewhere.

First you check the most obvious source, the Marriage Register of the New Credit Wesleyan Mission at the Archives of the United Church in Toronto. These records indicate that on 30 September 1877 Robert Sawyer, age 28, born at Owen Sound, living at New Credit, son of David and Anne Sawyer, married Lenia Young, age 16, living at New Credit, place of birth not given, daughter of John and Sarah Young. The same information could probably also be found in the Registrar General's records, but your clear indication of a place of residence made it very likely that New Credit was where the marriage took place. If you had less to go on, then using the Registrar General's indexes would have been a reasonable choice.

Now it will be of some importance to determine Lenia's tribal affiliation. You might assume that, due to her marriage, she will be on the pay lists of her tribe of origin until 1877, at which point she would have been listed with her husband at New Credit. It is also possible, however, that she would have been included with her parent's number, and her name might not appear, since she was only 16. However, you have heard from relatives that when Lenia married, both of her parents were dead, so you have some confidence that her name should exist separately in the listings.

You have a choice as to where to view the same records: at the Woodland Cultural Centre in Brantford, the National Archives in Ottawa or the Archives of Ontario in Toronto (or borrow the same on interlibrary loan from the Ottawa repository). You then systematically search the material, starting with 1878 (one year after the marriage), and proceed backwards. You find no entries for a Lenia (or variant spellings) Young under any of the tribal designations until the fall of 1876, when listed among the Lower Cayugas is Number 653, Magdeline Young. Lenia, Magdalene(a) and Madeline(a) are variants of the same name. This is the one and only time her name appears (you check back a few more years), which makes sense, since it is highly unlikely she would have been on a list by herself before age 13 or so. This individual seems to be an ideal candidate since there is no one else that fits the data, and her dropping off the records in 1877 is exactly what you had predicted.

Now, Magdeline was born about 1861, which may pose problems, since Ontario civil registration was not in effect at that time. As well, since she was a Lower Cayuga, her parents may not have been Christian and therefore she may not have been baptized. Also, referring to the census material might pose challenges, since the Cayugas were often listed only by their Native names. Unfortunately there is no Magdeline, John or Sarah Young listed in the 1871 personal census of the townships comprising the Reserve. However, referring to the end of the Tuscarora Township records, in the Deaths (in the previous year) list, we find that Sarah Young, a widow, age 26, born in the United States, "pagan" in religion, died in August of consumption. Therefore it seems that her husband, probably John Young, died before August 1870, and therefore, at age 10 or so, Magdeline was an orphan.

The 1861 Census of Tuscarora Township shows that on Lot 1, Concession 6, in one house lived Kayentatenh, age 71, a widow; John Young, a farmer, age 45; his wife, Sarah Young, age 20; and Niwadenhinraah, a male, age 20, single. All were of "no religion," meaning Longhouse faith. Unfortunately the census taker seems to have been very careless in noting places of birth, so the notation of "Upper Canada" for all must be taken with some reservations. Turning to the 1851 census, on the same lot and concession in this year is Kayendatye, age 75, a widow; Oghradonhkwen, a labourer, age 48, male, married; Shadina, age 37, male, married; Yonho-wenjenhawy, age 34, female, married; Deyohjikerakeh, age 28, male, single; Nihadenhenraha, age 10, male, single; plus six other single persons with only Native names. Obviously the ages, especially of the older individuals, must not be accepted uncritically.

A seemingly reasonable proposal would be that the above Shadina (1851) and John Young (1861) are the same individual. If so, Sarah would seem to be his second wife. Fortunately the issue can be answered by referring to the merchants' records for Alexander Scobie's store near Caledonia, where in 1851 and 1852 "John Young chief, Jadichna" appears. Clearly, from a phonetic perspective, the two names Shadina and Jadichna are likely identical (although the spelling, as was typical, differs). The suspicion is that John Young was Lower Cayuga (based on Magdeline's tribe of origin, since at this time persons were registered according to their father's tribe). Referring back to the pay lists, in the years between 1856 and 1859 the Lower Cayugas were listed only by their Native names. Here, in 1856 Shadinah has four in the family, but by 1857 the number had dropped to one. In 1861 the persons are now listed using their English names. In 1861 and 1862 John Young's grouping has him as the head of the family with one man, one woman and one child — a total of three. It appears that about 1859 John Young married Sarah, and by 1861 had a son (John, who also married at New Credit, in 1884, and is found listed next to Magdeline in the 1876 pay list). As expected, there is no girl listed with John Young, since Magdeline was apparently not born until 1861 or 1862. The paylist for 1863 indicates that four persons under the John Young listing were receiving monies. Again, the data is consistent with known facts and supports the contention that Magdeline was born in 1862.

A hypothesis that appears to fit with the data is that Kayendatye (1851 and 1861) is the widowed mother of John Young. It is now time to try to trace them to their former home, where they resided prior to the general migration to the present Six Nations Reserve in or about 1847. From reading my article on the various locations where the Lower Cayugas lived prior to 1847, it seems that the Young family probably resided near Willow Grove (between Caledonia and Hagersville) or along the Grand River at Indiana (Seneca Township) and Mount Healy (Oneida Township).[176] For this reason you searched among the collection of land papers relating to these townships and the Thorburn Diaries, looking for John Young (sometimes known as John Young chief) and his apparent mother, Kayendatye. In the papers relating to Oneida Township are records concerning the purchase by William Cook of the improvements of the Natives who resided on Lots 60 and 61, river lots, Oneida. For example, there is a receipt to "Lot No. 61 in the River Oneida which is mine having bought it from my brother 4 years ago," dated 4 October 1845, and signed by "John Young (his mark) Chief."[177] Another receipt dated 27 December 1845 was signed by "William (his mark) Young chief."[178] On 10 November 1843 Cook obtained the receipt from Gaiundadhe or "Chief's (her mark) wife" for lands she sold him in 1841,[179] and on 24 June 1847 "Gaiundahe (her mark)" provided Cook with a receipt for money he gave her for Lots 60 and 61.[180] Clearly Kayandatye and Gaiundadhe are phonetically the same.

We have now apparently traced Magdeline Sawyer's ancestry back in time to Mount Healy, where her father and grandparents lived until about 1845. Other items in this collection indicate that Kayandatye was known as "Big Squaw," and that in addition to John Young chief Shadina and William Young chief Tocanasago, she also had an unnamed son who died about 1838. Referring back to the 1851 census, it is likely that Oghradonkwen was also another son. He was probably the H. Young noted on Lot 1, Concession 6, Tuscarora in the Tremaine map of 1858, and the Henry Young chief found in a number of documents, one of which (a merchant's account) indicates that he died about 1858. It is, however, unlikely that much progress can be made in finding many further details about Young chief and his wife, Kayandatye. It is probable, however, that the "Young Chief" listed among the Lower Cayugas in the 1817 claims for losses incurred during the War of 1812 is John Young's father. This argument is more persuasive since Young Chief did not sign the receipt for the money received in 1837, perhaps because he was deceased at that time, which is implied by the data in the above land records.

Name Irregularities

The diverse spelling of names, particularly Native names, can make for significant difficulties. It will be necessary to use good phonetic skills to make comparisons. Spelling was highly variable and idiosyncratic. Problems arise when a name is written in one language (e.g., Cayuga) in one record, and in another Six Nations language (e.g., Mohawk) in a subsequent document. Furthermore, it was not unusual for Six Nations individuals to change names three times during their lives (e.g., when they accepted a chiefly title or were given the name of a deceased relative). If this wasn't problematic enough, sometimes a person was known by two (or more) prenames (e.g., Henry Aaron Hill was frequently noted as Aaron Henry Hill). Sometimes this was due to having two baptismal names, using the father's name as a middle name or changing names somewhere along the line. The Mohawk name for Margaret was (Kon)Wageri, and for Catharine was Kateri, and they might be transposed depending on likes or ability with the English language. Another difficulty is the possibility that a person could use two surnames, for reasons that are often obscure.

The 1871 census shows that living on River Lot 22, Tuscarora Township, was William House, age 35, born Ontario, member of the Church of England, an Oneida Indian, living with his wife Lucy, age 28, a Mohawk Indian, and six children, the eldest of whom was Mary, age 10. The Tuscarora Church records show that the couple married in 1860; he was an Onondaga and his wife, Lucy Walker, a Mohawk. Four of their children were baptized between 1860 and 1864 — the first was Mary, baptized 25 December 1860. Searching the 1861 census, there is no William House on the Reserve, but on Lot 22 is William Young, a farmer, born Upper Canada, member of the Church of England, age 22, with his wife Lucy, age 19, a female Betsey Turkey, age 8, and a female, Mary, age 4. The question is, are William House and William Young the same person?

The circumstantial evidence is very compelling, but it would be reassuring to have confirmation of the identification. Fortunately an unequivocal answer is available by referring to the merchant's records noted earlier. Here we find that in 1875 and 1876 Wm. House Yonge, a member of the Onondaga Clear Sky Band, owed money to Alexr. Smith.[181] Tracing William back to the 1851 census, it appears that he is the son of widow Ellen Young (an Oneida, according to the Mohawk Chapel church records), whose husband was John Young, a member of the St. Regis Band of Onondagas (according to the Six Nations census of 1849). It is unclear why William came to use the surname House (all later records are in this name), other than the possibility that his mother had the surname House (this is mere speculation).

Intermarriage

Native–Native

The census of 1871, as well as the various church records, indicate a broad tendency, increasing dramatically from the early years of the 1800s, to marry outside one's own nation or tribal group, for example, a Tuscarora man marrying a Seneca woman. In addition, there are many examples that highlight the flow of Native people to and from the Reserve. The various censuses of Ontario confirm the frequency of this behaviour, highlighted by the number of persons then resident on the Reserve who were born, for example, in Buffalo. There seemed to have been a particular link with the Muncey Reserve on the Thames River, the Bay of Quinte Tyendinaga Reserve, a Wyandotte Reserve and, of course, the nearby New Credit Reserve.

Native–Non-Native

Another phenomenon was "racial" mixing, involving marriages between Natives and both Whites and Blacks. Probably many of the readers of this book suspect that they have some family connection to the Six Nations tribes, but have not yet established this link. Many of the non-Native (White/Euro-Canadian and Black/African Canadian) men who married Six Nations women chose to live on the Reserve with their wives and raise their children there. Some of their descendants, however, did have a tendency to marry out and join the general Canadian community.

There were also many non-Native men who married Six Nations women and lived off the Reserve. Their children frequently blended into the surrounding culture and became indistinguishable from their Euro-Canadian neighbours. Their descendants tended to spread out across North America, and may or may not have even the slightest notion about their distant Six Nations heritage. The chart on pages 84–85 is provided to assist these individuals. It is a list of all the marriages known to have taken place between a non-Native man and a Six Nations woman. Although there were also Six Nations men who married White women, their descendants tended to merge into the Reserve community, so their families would by and large emerge through a study of the records described earlier.

In addition, the records indicate that the following Black/African-Canadian males also married Six Nations women: Peter Barton, Prime Hill, — Jackson, John Morey, Vincent Settles and probably Prince VanPatter.

White Men and Their Six Nations Wives, 1740–1870

	Husband's Name	Approx. Date of Marriage	Wife's Name or Family	Wife's Tribe
1.	Abel ACKLEY	1870	unknown	unknown
2.	Wm. ARMSTRONG	1835	Eliza. FUNN	Oneida
3.	George BRADLEY	1865	Hannah	Mohawk
4.	Chauncey BURNHAM	1800	Mary DOCHSTADER	Cayuga (h)
5.	Chauncey BURNHAM	1803	Catherine DOCHSTADER	Onondaga (h)
6.	Lyman BURNHAM	1807	Catherine DOCHSTADER	Onondaga (h)
7.	Oliver BURNHAM	1808	Catherine HUFF	Delaware (h)
8.	William CALDWELL	1782	dau. of Flying Sun	Mohawk
9.	John CAMP		unknown	Mohawk or Cayuga
10	Ralfe CLENCH	1793	Elizabeth JOHNSON	Mohawk (h)
11.	Nicholas COTTER	1790	Margaret	Mohawk
12.	John CROKER	1818	Mary THOMPSON	Delaware (h)
13.	Robert Hill DEE	1856	Elizabeth (SMITH?)	Mohawk
14.	John DOCHSTADER (Sr.)	1780	unknown	Cayuga
15.	John DOCHSTADER (Sr.)	1785	niece of Kaneahintwaghte	Onondaga
16.	John DOCHSTADER (Jr.)	1790	Catherine	Delaware
17.	Wm. DOCHSTADER	1815	Hannah DENNIS	Delaware (h)
18.	John DUNCAN	1861	Christiana	Cayuga
19.	William ELLIOTT	1855	Margaret JOHNSON	Mohawk
20.	Robert ENNIS	1800	Sarah	Mohawk
21.	Isaac EVERITT	1858	Hester ADAMS	Mohawk
22.	Isaac EVERLAU	1847	Lydia HILL	Mohawk
23.	Robert C. FENNESY	1851	Catharine	Mohawk
24.	Wil. FRADENBURGH	1820	Sarah DOCHSTADER	Delaware (h)
25.	Thomas GOOD	1870	Julia (BOMBERRY?)	Mohawk
26.	Robert HARPER	1833	Betsy OWEN	Tuscarora
27.	John HUFF	1780	unknown	Delaware
28.	Yankee JOHN	1800	unknown	Mohawk
29.	Sir Wm. JOHNSON	1740	unknown	Mohawk

White Men and Their Six Nations Wives, 1740–1870 (*Concluded*)

	Husband's Name	Approx. Date of Marriage	Wife's Name or Family	Wife's Tribe
30.	Sir Wm. JOHNSON	1755	Mary BRANT	Mohawk
31.	Augustus JONES	1798	Sarah TEKARIHOGEN	Mohawk
32.	Robert KERR	1780	Elizabeth JOHNSON	Mohawk (h)
33.	William KERBY	1810	Margaret SMITH	Mohawk (h)
34.	John J. LEFFERTY	1800	Mary JOHNSON	Mohawk (h)
35.	Henry LICKERS	1800	unknown	Mohawk
36.	Henry MARACLE	1783	unknown	Mohawk
37.	Daniel MCNAUGHTON	1861	Mary (LEWIS?)	Cayuga
38.	Anthony MILLER	1863	Sarah DOCHSTADER	Mohawk
39.	George MURDOCK	1846	Betsy SILVERSMITH	Onondaga
40.	Warner NELLES	1796	Elizabeth YOUNG	Mohawk (h)
41.	James PARKER	1825	Rachel JONES	Mohawk (h)
42.	Epaph. L. PHELPS	1795	Esther HILL	Mohawk
43.	Julianne POUDRC(?)	1844	Mary ISAAC	Onondaga
44.	William RUGGLES	1823	Sarah JOHNSON	Mohawk (h)
45.	Archibald RUSSELL	1825	Catherine JONES	Mohawk (h)
46.	George SCOTT	1858	Lucinda	Mohawk
47.	Wm. Kennedy SMITH	1790	Mary HILL	Mohawk
48.	Alexander STEWART	1796	Jemima JOHNSON	Mohawk (h)
49.	John THOMAS	1845	Hester JOHN	Mohawk
50.	James VIAS	1865	Phebe Ann (WALKER?)	Mohawk
51.	George WHIGHT	1850	Mary	Onondaga
52.	John YOUNG	1765	Catherine HILL	Mohawk

This table is a skeletal summary of *documented* marriages between White/Euro-Canadian males and Six Nations (of the Grand River) females. To be included, the man and/or the woman must have resided in Ontario. Half-Native males such as John Norton (half Cherokee) are not included. The definition of "Native woman" here includes those who had only one Six Nations parent (they were half White), noted with an "h" after the tribal name in the chart. The data are compiled from the sources noted previously in this book.

Sons of some of the people in the chart on pages 84–85. Portrait of
Rev. Peter Jones Kahkewaquonaby, son of Augustus Jones and
Tuhbenahnequay, b. 1802, ½ Mississauga. Brant County Museum and
Archives, (S136/1-2). Acc. 974.24.5.

Portrait of A.K. Smith, son of William K. Smith and Mary Hill. Painting attributed to Whale, Brant County Museum and Archives (SSA 66). Acc. X977.4. Photo by D.K.Faux

Major Repositories

The following list includes the names and contact information of the repositories most useful to the study of Six Nations of Ontario genealogy. Additional details include a general overview of their primary collections and suggestions as to how to maximize your success with their records. Every effort has been made to ascertain the accuracy of this information up to the date of publication.

Archives

National Archives of Canada
395 Wellington Street
Ottawa, Ontario
K1A 0N3
Tel.: 1-866-578-7777
www.archives.ca

The collections housed here, primarily the RG 10 Indian Affairs Papers, are the single most important source for those researching Native genealogies. Fortunately, many of the most useful sources have been microfilmed, and are available not only here but also at the Archives of Ontario.

Archives of Ontario
77 Grenville Street
Toronto, Ontario
M5S 1B3
Tel.: 416-327-1600
1-800-668-9933 (Ontario only)
www.archives.gov.on.ca

Those with easier access to Toronto than Ottawa will be able to find many of the important RG 10 Indian Affairs Papers and other records from the NA (for example, the Claus Papers) on microfilm at the AO. In addition, there are a number of unique items here (e.g., the Norton Papers).

United Church of Canada Central Archives
Victoria University
73 Queen's Park Crescent East
Toronto, Ontario
M5S 1K7
Tel.: 416-585-4563
www.united-church.ca/archives

Anglican Diocese of Huron Synod Archives
Huron University College Library
University of Western Ontario
1349 Western Road
London, Ontario
N6G 1H3
Tel.: 519-645-7956
www.huronuc.on.ca/library&computing

Anglican Diocese of Niagara Synod Archives
Special Collections
Mills Memorial Library
McMaster University
1280 Main Street West
Hamilton, Ontario
L8S 4L6
Tel.: 905-525-9140, ext. 22010
www.mcmaster.ca/library/mills/mills.htm

Montgomery County Department of History and Archives
New County Office Building
P.O. Box 1500
Broadway
Fonda, N.Y. 12068-1500
U.S.A.
Tel.: 518-853-8115
www.amsterdam-ny.com/mcha

Sources on the Six Nations Reserve

Indian and Northern Affairs Canada
Brantford District Office
Brantford Business Centre
58 Dalhousie St., 3rd Floor
P.O. Box 1960
Brantford, Ontario
N3T 5W5
Tel.: 519-751-2200
www.ainc-inac.gc.ca/on/index_e.html

Six Nations Membership Office
Six Nations Council
67 Bicentennial Trail
P.O. Box 62
Ohsweken, Ontario
N0A 1M0
Tel.: 519-445-4613
www.sixnations.ca

This is a very convenient and efficient way to check for details (band number, tribe, birth and death dates, family relationships) of individuals who were registered Six Nations members anywhere from the late 1880s to the present. The Council's purpose is to assist applicants in obtaining status as a Six Nations member. This repository has an index card system that allows the staff to access material for you in a matter of a few minutes. You will be charged a fee for longer, more detailed searches. However, if status is proved, there is no cost. Janice G. Martin is the Membership Manager at the time of writing, and Mark Hill the Researcher.

Six Nations Records Management Centre
Six Nations Council
4th Line
Ohsweken, Ontario
N0A 1M0
Tel.: 519-445-2712

This office has on site an extensive set of microfilm copies of records that were once housed in the Indian Affairs Office in Brantford. In essence, their collections complement those in the Indian Affairs Papers at the NA. Apparently in the 1960s, while the records from the Brantford Indian Affairs Office were being transferred to the NA, a local genealogist complained that this would unduly restrict local people's access to these records. Therefore those records that remained were left in Brantford pending a decision as to what was the next course of action. Apparently in the meanwhile the Six Nations Council decided that these documents belonged to the Council, and so stopped all access. They were then microfilmed, and the microfilms placed at the Records Centre. What this means is that there are many important records here, but their access is still restricted. To have any free access to the documents you must obtain a Band Council resolution from the Six Nations Council. You will probably not be successful.

Another option is to have the Records staff do a search on your behalf as long as you can provide a good reason for wanting information from these records. You will need to fill out an application form giving your reasons for wanting information from the records and specifying how much time you authorize for the search. The staff members appear to be quite reasonable in assessing these requests. If they approve your application, you will be given two free hours of staff search time, with the remaining time charged at $12 per hour. Photocopies can be made at a cost of $1.25 per copy. The search time can take months because of the priorities of that setting (Band Council work takes precedence). Anne Scott is the Archivist.

The collection includes pay lists, Council minutes and census material dating from 1834 to the present, school records (e.g., Mohawk Institute), letter books and registers from 1845, land papers from 1830, voters' lists, adoption records, hospital files and sundry materials such as records concerning members of the Six Nations living in the United States 1881–1886.

Woodland Cultural Centre
184 Mohawk Street
Brantford, Ontario
N3T 5V6
Tel.: 519-759-2650
www.woodland-centre.on.ca

This repository has perhaps the most complete collection of difficult-to-obtain books and manuscripts. More recent publications are on open stacks and the older and more fragile publications are in locked cabinets in a restricted access (Archives) room. Also open for casual inspection is the Vertical File Collection, housing a diverse collection of materials including photocopied church registers and pamphlets on every conceivable aspect of Six Nations history and culture. The Archives room also houses microfilm copies of many useful items, much of it from the NA (e.g., pay lists 1856–1888). The Researcher, Sheila Staats, is a key resource person in the community and can direct individuals to those involved in related or pertinent projects (e.g., those researching clan names). Winnie Jacobs is the Librarian. Tom Hill, the Director, is involved in many projects (e.g., social history) and has a particular interest in Six Nations artistic endeavours.

Libraries

McMaster University
Mills Memorial Library
1280 Main Street West
Hamilton, Ontario
L8S 4L6
Tel.: 905-525-9140, ext. 220101

In addition to the Ontario census 1842–1901 and sundry books on Six Nations (listed under "Iroquois") people, McMaster also has important items such as the published Marriage Register collection for all the counties of Ontario. Also of particular significance is the fact that they have the entire set of Haldimand Papers and those from the Society for the Propagation of the Gospel in Foreign Parts.

Brantford Public Library
173 Colborne Street
Brantford, Ontario
N3T 2G8
Tel.: 519-756-2220
www.brantford.library.on.ca

On the lower level of this very modern library in the Reference Section is a small locked area housing the Ontario Genealogical Society Collection. Ask a librarian at the Reference Desk for access to this collection. Your first task should be to locate the binder entitled "Guide to the Local History Collection Brantford Public Library — Six Nations." This research tool provides a comprehensive guide to their collection of books, pamphlets, articles and newspaper clippings. Here you will find, for example, binders containing cemetery records. This area also houses hanging files with computer printouts of births, marriages and deaths from the *Brantford Weekly Expositor* 1852–1930. The library also has copies of the Brant County Census from 1851 to 1901. In the general Reference Section area is a card index file entitled "Local History" that includes sundry entries by surname.

Hamilton Public Library
Central Library
Special Collections and Archives
55 York Boulevard
Hamilton, Ontario
L8N 4E4
Tel.: 905-546-3408
www.hpl.ca

In their Special Collections and Archives section this library has a complete set of the Ontario census. In addition, they have a wide selection of genealogically relevant materials. While there, it would be worthwhile to check their card index under subject and surname.

Family History Centre
Church of Jesus Christ of Latter Day Saints
701 Stonechurch Road East
Hamilton, Ontario
L8W 1A9
Tel.: 905-385-5009
www.familysearch.org

This is an important resource centre with dedicated and knowledge-able volunteers to assist. All people are welcome. Their vast records on microfilm are worth checking under surnames of interest. It is possible that someone in the world has researched your family and submitted the records to the Temple for "sealing" as part of his or her religious duties. Here you can find microfilm copies of the available Ontario civil registrations from the Registrar of Ontario. They also have on site many records relating to Haldimand and Brant counties (e.g., marriage registers, census, wills). You can also order microfilm copies of many records that are otherwise difficult to access, for example, Church Registers of St. John's Tuscarora.

Toronto Public Library
Central Reference Library
789 Yonge Street
Toronto, Ontario
M4W 2G8
Tel.: 416-395-5577
www.tpl.toronto.on.ca

Museums

Brant County Museum and Archives
57 Charlotte Street
Brantford, Ontario
N3T 2W6
Tel.: 519-752-2483
www.bfree.on.ca/comdir/musgal/bcma

Joseph Brant Museum
1240 North Shore Blvd. East
Burlington, Ontario
L7S 1C5
Tel.: 905-634-3556
www.geocities.com/burlington_museums

Eva Brook Donly Museum
109 Norfolk Street South
Simcoe, Ontario
N3Y 2W3
Tel.: 519-426-1583
www.norfolklore.com/

Canadian Museum of Civilization
100 Laurier Street
P.O. Box 3100, Stn. B
Hull, Quebec
J8X 4H2
Tel.: 819-776-7000
www.civilization.ca

Registrars

Office of the Registrar General of Ontario
189 Red River Road, 3rd Floor
P.O. Box 4600
Thunder Bay, Ontario
P7B 6L8
1-800-461-2156
or
900 Bay Street, Room M2/49
MacDonald Block
Parliament Buildings
Toronto, Ontario
M7A 1X5
416-325-8305 (for 416 and 905 local calls)
www.cbs.gov.on.ca/mcbs

Registrar, Indian Registration
Indian and Northern Affairs
10 Wellington Street, North Tower
Hull, Quebec
Postal Address
Ottawa, Ontario
K1A 0H4
Tel.: 819-997-0380
Fax: 819-953-3017
www.ainc-inac.gc.ca

Other

Surveyor General of Ontario
Ministry of Natural Resources
Geographic Information Ontario
Robinson Place, 2nd Floor, N.
300 Water Street
P.O. Box 7000
Peterborough, Ontario
K9J 8M5
Tel.: 705-755-2204
www.mnr.gov.on.ca/MNR

Grace Anglican Church
15 Albion Street
Brantford, Ontario
N3T 3L9
Tel.: 519-752-6814
www.brant.net/graceanglican

Cornplanter's Descendants Association
Jack Ericson
Archivist and Genealogist
Special Collections
Reed Library
State University of New York College at Fredonia
Fredonia, NY 14063
USA
Tel.: 716-673-3183
www.fredonia.edu/library

Notes

1 David Faux. "Documenting Six Nations Indian Ancestry," *Families*, Vol. 20, No. 1 (1981), pp. 31–42.
2 Indian Affairs and Northern Development, Federal Building, Brantford, Ontario.
3 *Records Relating to Indian Affairs, Public Affairs Division General Inventory Series, RG 10* (Ottawa: Indian and Northern Affairs, 1975).
4 G. Elmore Reaman. *The Trail of the Iroquois Indians* (Toronto: Peter Martin Assoc., 1967), pp. 113–125.
5 Museum of the Woodland Cultural Centre, Brantford, Ontario. See Appendix.
6 NA. RG 10, Vols. 9563–9568, Interest and Distribution Pay Lists 1856–1888 (microfilm C-7177).
7 NA. Manpower and Social Development Records Section, Public Records Division, will forward applications to the Department of Indian Affairs and Northern Development, Treaties and Historical Research Division.
8 NA. RG 10, Vol. 223, Census of 1856, pp. 132530j–132530ff.
9 Ibid. Vol 851, Census of 1864, pp. 631–660.
10 Geo. C. Tremaine. *Tremaine's Map of the County of Brant* (New York: Tremaine, 1858).
11 Charles Pelham Mulvany. *History of Brant County of Ontario* (Toronto: Warner, Beers, 1883), pp. 643–644, 686–689.
12 John Noon. *Law and Government of the Grand River Iroquois* (New York: Viking, 1949).
13 New York (State) Legislature. Senate Committee on Indian Affairs. Testimony taken Before the Senate Committee on Indian Affairs Relative to the Cayuga Indians Under Resolution of May 15, 1889. Transmitted to the Legislature May 9, 1890. (New York State Senate Document No. 58). (Albany: J.B. Lyon).

14 Anglican Diocese of Huron, London. Registers of the Anglican Church of St. John's, Tuscarora Township, from 1829.

15 Brant County Museum. Registers of the Mohawk Church (Luard Transcripts), 1827–1877.

16 Archives of Ontario (AO), Marriage Registers Collection Marriage Register of the New Credit Wesleyan Mission.

17 United Church Archives. Methodist Baptismal Register 1834–1874, Tuscarora Township.

18 a. AO. Haldimand County Marriage Register 1858–1869. b. AO. Brant County Marriage Register 1858–1868. AO. MSS. Misc. Coll. 1789, No. 1.

19 C.M. Johnston. *Valley of the Six Nations* (Toronto: University of Toronto Press, 1968). See also *Journal of the Legislative Assembly*, Appendix GGG, Province of Canada, 2nd Part, 1st Session, Vol. 4, No. 2, 1844–1845 for pay lists of Indian claimants for losses during the War of 1812.

20 NA. RG 10, Vol. 140, 1843 Property Census, pp. 170322–170340 (microfilm C-11490), and Vol. 999A, Census for Presents, 1847–1852.

21 NA. RG 10, Vols. 896–906, Accounts, Six Nations Superintendency, 1844–1880.

22 For example: NA. RG 10, Vol. 27, Council 5 March 1809, pp. 15858–15867, and Vol. 144, Council 18 December, 1844, pp. 83274–83276.

23 NA. RG 10, Vols. 103–113, Grand River Claims 1788–1844 (microfilm C-11472–11477) and Vols. 803–893, Correspondence, Six Nations Superintendency, 1809–1899.

24 NA, RG 10, Vols. 727–734 (microfilm C-13413–13417).

25 AO. Nelles Family Papers 1780–1866.

26 AO. Norton Papers 1796–1843.

27 NA. Brant Family Papers 1774–1874, MG 19, F6 (microfilm C-6818).

28 NA. Claus Papers MG 19, F1 (microfilm C-1478–1485).

29 AO. Thorburn Papers 1845–1874. Diaries, Six Nations Indians.

30 Lyman Draper. MSS, University of Wisconsin, Madison. See especially F, Vols 13–14.

31 *Papers and Records of the Ontario Historical Society*. Vol. 1, pp. 133–117 and Vol. 12, pp. 96–101.

32 Barbara Graymont. *The Iroquois in the American Revolution* (Syracuse: Syracuse University Press, 1972).

33 NA. Sir Frederick Haldimand Transcripts, Unpublished Papers and Correspondence 175801784, MG 21.

34 NA. Q Series, CO 42, Vol. 47, from p. 240 and Vol. 24, Pt. 2, from p. 307.

35 Society for the Propagation of the Gospel in Foreign Parts, London, England, Letterbooks Series A, Vols. 8–13, 1702–1737.

36 Rev. Henry Barclay. Register of Marriages, Baptisms, Communicants, and Burials Among the Mohawk Indians, 26 January 1735 to 16 February 1746. Transcripts are available at the Montgomery County Archives, Fonda, New York. See the Appendix.

37 Rev. John Ogilvie. A Register of Indian Children, 22 April 1750 to 11 February 1759. Transcripts are available at the Archives of the State of New York, Albany.

38 Richmond P. Bond. *Queen Anne's American Kings* (New York: Octagon, 1974). The original paintings are now in the possession of the National Archives of Canada.

39 Sir William Johnson. *The Papers of Sir William Johnson*, ed. by James Sullivan et al. (13 Vols.) Albany, from 1921.

40 Ibid. Vol. 13. pp. 172–178.

41 NA. MG 19, F 26, *Cosmogony of DeKanawidas Government of the Iroquois Confederacy: The Original Literal Historical Narratives of the Iroquois Confederacy*, by Seth Newhouse (1885).

42 Edward S. Rogers and Donald B. Smith, eds. *Aboriginal Ontario: Historical Perspectives on the First Nations* (Toronto: Dundurn Press, 1994).

43 Bruce G. Trigger, ed. *Handbook of North American Indians: Northeast*, Vol. 15 (Washington: Smithsonian Institution, 1978).

44 Edward M. Chadwick. *The People of the Longhouse* (London: Church of England Publishing, 1897).

45 Charles M. Johnston. *The Valley of the Six Nations: A Collection of Documents on the Indian Lands of the Grand River* (Toronto: Champlain Society, 1964).

46 Government of Canada. *1991 Census of Canada* (Ottawa: Statistics Canada, 1993).

47 *Records Relating to Indian Affairs, Public Affairs Division General Inventory Series, RG 10* (Ottawa: Indian and Northern Affairs, 1975).

48 Bill Russell. *Records of the Federal Department of Indian Affairs at the National Archives of Canada: A Source for Genealogical Research* (Toronto: The Ontario Genealogical Society, 1998). This publication is a companion to the present work, and is especially useful for anyone researching ancestors in the late nineteenth and early twentieth centuries.

49 Bennett Ellen McCardle. *Indian History and Claims: A Research*

Handbook. Vol. 1, *Research Projects*; Vol. 2, *Research Methods* (Ottawa: Indian and Northern Affairs Canada, 1982).

50 James Morrison. *First Nations in the Archives: A Guide to Aboriginal Sources at the Archives of Ontario* (Toronto: Archives of Ontario/ Ministry of Culture and Communication, 1992).

51 Brenda Dougall Merriman. *Genealogy in Ontario: Searching the Records* (3d ed.) (Toronto: Ontario Genealogical Society, 1996). This publication is the most definitive available study of, and practical guide to, general Ontario genealogical records and sources.

52 Robert Lochiel Fraser. "George Powlis," in F.G. Halpenny, ed., *Dictionary of Canadian Biography* Vol. 7, 1851–1860 (Toronto: University of Toronto Press, 1985), pp. 707–709.

53 Merriman, pp. viii–xiv.

54 *The Haldimand Tribune*, Vol. 3, No. 12, Thursday 23 January 1862.

55 AO. RG 22 05/122/022, Box 48, Criminal Indictments, Haldimand County. Joseph Latham, 1862.

56 NA. RG 10, Vol. 814. Letter from Hannah Dochstader to David Thorburn, 19 June 1845, p. 654.

57 Ibid. Certificate from James Winniett, 18 June 1845, p. 656.

58 Ibid. Vol. 999A.

59 Department of Indian Affairs and Northern Development. *Basic Departmental Data for 1992* (Ottawa: Department of Supply and Services, 1992).

60 NA. RG 10, Vol. 108, Pt. 1. Letter from Jas Winnett, 4 April 1835, p. 419, (microfilm C-11474).

61 Noon.

62 Department of Indian Affairs and Northern Development. *Identification and Registration of Indian and Inuit People* (Ottawa: Department of Supply and Services, 1993).

63 Lynn A. Morgan, ed. *Loyalist Lineages of Canada: 1783–1983* (Agincourt, Ontario: Generation Press, 1984).

64 Peter B. Merey. *Loyalist Families of the Grand River Branch, United Empire Loyalists' Association of Canada* (Toronto: Pro Familia Publishing, 1991).

65 Edward M. Chadwick. *Ontarian Families: Genealogies of United Empire Loyalists and Other Pioneer Families of Upper Canada* (Lambertville, New Jersey: Hunterdon House, 1970; reprint of 1894 edition).

66 Francess G. Halpenny, gen. ed. *Dictionary of Canadian Biography* (Toronto: University of Toronto Press). There are thirteen volumes in this series. See Index (1991).

67 Reaman.

68 Mulvany, pp. 643–644, 686–689.

69 Isabel Thompson Kelsay. *Joseph Brant (1743–1807): A Man of Two Worlds* (Syracuse: Syracuse University Press, 1984).

70 J. Ojijatekha Brant-Sero. "Some Descendants of Joseph Brant," *Papers and Records of the Ontario Historical Society*, Vol. 1, pp. 113–117.

71 Gordon J. Smith. "Capt. Joseph Brant's Status as a Chief, and Some of his Descendants," *Papers and Records of the Ontario Historical Society*, Vol. 12, pp. 89–101.

72 Registrar General of Ontario (see Appendix for address). Their birth, marriage and death records commence on 1 July 1869. There are extensive discussions of their contents in most Ontario genealogical guides.

73 AO. RG 8, Series I-6-A (now RG 80-27-1), District Marriage Register Collections, Gore District (1842–1855) (microfilm #MS 248, Reel 2).

74 AO. RG 8, Series 1-6-B (now RG80-27-2), County Marriage Register Collections, Haldimand County (1858–1869) and Brant County (1859–1869). These items are redily available in published versions (see note 75).

75 Libby Hancocks. *County Marriage Registers of Ontario, Canada: 1858–1869*, Vol. 21, *Haldimand County* and Vol. 22, *Brant County* (Agincourt, Ontario: Generation Press, 1989).

76 Janet Carnochan. "Early Records of St. Mark's and St. Andrew's Churches, Niagara," *Papers and Records of the Ontario Historical Society*, Vol. 3, (1901), pp. 7–85.

77 Brant County Branch (BCB) Ontario Genealogical Society. *Registery of the Mohawk Chapel, 1827–1943; Births, Marriages, Burials.* Publication Number 186-190, 200.

78 State Historical Society of Wisconsin (Madison), Brant Miscellanies, Lyman Draper Collection, Vol. 13, Series F, pp. 58–59.

79 Archives of the Diocese of Huron, Huron College (see Appendix for more information).

80 LDS. Registers of St. John's Church, Tuscarora (microfilm #1015812).

81 WCC. "Registers of St. John's Church, Tuscarora (1867–1914)." Photocopies found in a folder in the Vertical File Collection under the heading "Six Nations."

82 WCC. "Baptismal Register of St. Luke's Church, Delaware (Six Nations)." This item is a photocopy, contained in a folder in the Vertical File Collection in the General Reading Room.

83 Elizabeth Graham. *Medicine Man to Missionary: Missionaries as*

Agents of Change among the Indians of Southern Ontario, 1784–1867 (Toronto: Peter Martin Assoc., 1975).

84 AO. RG 8, Series I-6-A (ms 248), Marriage Registers Collection. Marriage Register of the New Credit Wesleyan Mission (microfim 2.3).

85 AUC. Hamilton Conference, Brant Presbytery, New Credit, Ontario, Mission. "Members of the Methodist Society of the Upper Mohawks. Grand River. January 10, 1826." These records are on microfilm.

86 AUC. Wesleyan Methodist Baptismal Register, 1834–1874. These records are on microfilm, and can be accessed by using indices to townships. They show the child's name, date and place of birth and baptism, along with the parents' names (without birth surname) and their residence.

87 BCB. Publication Numbers 63, 109–128 and 133. Note that the vast majority of these tombstones date from the 1880s to the present.

88 NA. Census Returns 1666–1901, Province of Ontario. Microfilm copies have been widely distributed, and most repositories provide finding aids.

89 Merriman.

90 Toni Jollay Prevost. *Indians from New York in Ontario and Quebec, Canada: A Genealogy Reference*, Vol. 2 (Bowie, Maryland: Heritage Books, 1995).

91 NA. RG 10, Vol. 803, Pt. 1, "Distribution of the Sum of £1500 Among the People of the Six Nations on the Grand River," *circa* 1838, begins p. 143.

92 NA. RG 10, Vols. 9563–9568, "Interest Distribution Pay Lists: Six Nations," 1856–1888 (microfilm C-7177).

93 Johnston, p. 52.

94 NA. RG 10, Vol. 41, "The Return of the Number of the Upper Mohawks, Men, Women and Children, in This Season," 31 July 1823, pp. 22349-22351 (microfilm C-11012).

95 NA. RG 10, Vol. 58, "Nominal List of the Mohawk Indians of the Bay of Quinte, who left there last Spring and came and settled on the Grand River," 1 December 1835, p. 59534 and Vol. 59, pp. 60262 and 60399.

96 NA. RG 10, Vol. 140, "List of Six Nations Property in A.D. 1843," pp. 170322–170340 (microfilm C-11490).

97 NA. RG 10, Vol. 999A, "General Return of the Six Nations Entitled to Presents for the Year 1849"; Ibid. 1850; Ibid. 1852.

98 NA. RG 10, Vol. 223, "Census Return of Indians Under the Superintendence of David Thorburn Esq.," 23 February 1856, pp. 132539j–132530ff.

99 NA. RG 10, Vol. 851, "Census List of Six Nations Indians for 1864," pp. 631–660.

100 NA. RG 10, Vols. 103–113, "Grand River Claims 1788–1844." (microfilm C-11472–11477); Vols. 803–893, "Correspondence, Six Nations Superintendency, 1844–1880."

101 New York Historical Society. "Miscl. Lansing, John Jr., Power of Attorney to Jelles Fonda to Recover Lands Granted to Abraham Van Horne and others Nov. 13, 1731." Located in catalogue under "Indians, Mohawks."

102 NA. MG 19, F21, "Treaty between the Indians formerly resident at the Mohawk Castle ... and the State of New York."

103 NA. RG 10, Vol. 42, "Principal Chiefs or Sachems of the Six Nations, to William Kennedy Smith," 25 August 1824, p. 22614 (microfilm C-11013).

104 NA. RG 10, Vol. 123, "Petition of William Kennedy Smith," 14 October 1847, pp. 6287–6288 (microfilm C-11481).

105 State Historical Society of Wisconsin (Madison), Brant Miscellanies, Lyman Draper Collection, Series F, Vol. 14, pp. 38–39 and pp. 75–77.

106 NA. RG 10. Some volumes of particular interest here are 103–113, 119–121 and 803.

107 NA. RG 10, Land Inspection Returns. One example here is the Oneida Township records in Vol. 157 (microfilm C-11497).

108 NA. RG 10, Vol. 151, pp. 87568–87597.

109 David Faux. "Lower Cayuga Settlements Prior to 1850: Documentary Evidence," *KEWA*, Newsletter of the London Chapter of the Ontario Archaeological Society (Sept. 1985), pp. 6–24.

110 Tremaine.

111 H.R. Page. *Illustrated Historical Atlas of the County of Brant* (Toronto: Page & Smith, 1875).

112 NA. RG 10, Vol. 803, Pt. 2, 21 September 1836, pp. 427–428 (microfilm C-15103).

113 Surveyor General of Ontario Thomas Parke map. "Showing the Indian improvements on the River lots at Tuscarora. June 1843," Map #10759, E-2.

114 NA. RG 10, Vol. 27, "Minutes of a Council, Onondaga, Grand River, 9 November 1806," pp. 15670–15676 (microfilm C-11007).

115 NA. RG 10, Vol. 111, p. 273 and Vol. 121–122, 147.

116 NA. RG 10, "Index to the Red Series." (microfilm C-15713). This reel is also found at WCC. These records date from the 1880s to the 1920s, and have recently been removed from the restricted list.

117 NA. RG 10, Red Series, Vol. 2315, File #62,615. "Letter from J. Gilki-
     son Superintendent of the Six Nations to the Superintendent General
     of Indian Affairs Concerning the Right of Mrs. John Cayuga to Live
     on the Reserve, 18 September 1885." (microfilm C-12781R).

118 Noon, p. 182.

119 NA. RG 10, Vol. 2. Letter from David Price, Interpreter, Ft. George,
     30 January 1807, p. 557 (microfilm C-10996).

120 Ibid. "Jos. Kemp et al. to Mr. St. John, Grand River, 18 March 1807,"
     p. 559.

121 NA. RG 10, Vol. 6. Petition of Margaret Powles et al. to Lord Sydenham,
     Brantford, 14 May 1841, pp. 2708–2724.

122 NA. RG 10, Vol. 139, Pt. 1. "List of Lower Cayuga Indians, living near
     Indiana Grand River, who signed a petition to the Governor General
     in the Spring 1843," p. 70735.

123 NA. Colonial Office Records, Q Series, Vol. 24, Pt. 2, pp. 307–325.

124 NA. MG 11, CO 42, Vol. 47, pp. 240–242.

125 New York State Archives. Assembly Papers, Vol. 40, pp. 41–44.

126 Journal of the Legislative Assembly, Appendix GGG, Province of
     Canada, 2nd Part, 1st Session, Vol. 4, No. 2, 1844–1845. Pay lists of
     Indian claimants for losses during the War of 1812

127 New York (State) Legislature. Senate Committee on Indian Affairs.
     Testimony taken Before the Senate Committee on Indian Affairs
     Relative to the Cayuga Indians Under Resolution of May 15, 1889.
     Transmitted to the Legislature May 9, 1890. (New York State Senate
     Document No. 58). (Albany: J.B. Lyon), p. 57, 269.

128 Sir Frederick Haldimand Unpublished Papers and Correspondence
     1758–1784. The most useful reels appear to be 32 to 52, 79 to 93 and
     109 to 110. There is a printed finding aid, but no index. Transcripts
     of these records (some indexed) are found at the NA. MG 21, Vols.
     B100 to B167.

129 Ibid. Reel 58, Add. MSS. 21787, p. 186.

130 Ibid. Reel 51, Add. MSS. 21774, p. 160.

131 Johnston, pp. 203–205.

132 NA. MG 19, F1, Claus Papers. "List of the Prinsible Chiefs and war
     Chiefs of the Six Nation, Grand River, 22 February 1815," Vol. 10,
     pp. 153–156.

133 NA. RG 10, Vol. 29, p. 17367 (microfilm C-11008).

134 AO. MS 94, John Norton Papers 1796–1843. "List of Mohawks who
     receive rations," undated (circa 1814).

135 NA. RG 10, C Series, Vol. 261. "List of Chiefs and principal warriors,

whose conduct through the war has deserved approbation," John Norton, 13 February 1817, pp. 25–29.

136 NA. MG 19, F1, Claus Papers (microfilms C-1478–1485).

137 NA. MG 19, F6, Brant Family Papers 1774–1874 (microfilm C-6818).

138 NA. MG 30, C 169, Elliott Moses Papers 1846–1975. Elliott Moses was a Delaware historian and kept extensive records on all manner of subjects relating to the Six Nations.

139 AO. John Norton Papers 1796–1843.

140 AO. MU 2986, David Thorburn Papers 1845–1862. Diaries, Six Nations Indians.

141 NA. MG 19, F1, Claus Papers. Vol. 4, pp. 79–81; Vol. 24, pp. 24–25.

142 Annmarie Anrod Shimony. *Conservatism among the Iroquois at the Six Nations Reserve* (Syracuse University Press: Syracuse, 1994; reprint of 1961 edition, with index).

143 Canadian Museum of Civilization. Unpublished manuscripts of A.A. Goldenweiser. Goldenweiser Note Books, #28, Mohawk Names. There is in existence a manuscript entitled "Iroquois Notes. Table of Contents" that includes a listing of the contents of his 29 fieldbooks. The only identification is a set of code numbers on this document: 1252.1, B179F5, 111-1-62M, part 1.

144 William N. Fenton. *Role Call of the Iroquois Chiefs: A Study of a Mnemonic Cane from the Six Nations Reserve*, (Washington: Smithsonian Institution, 1950).

145 Lewis Henry Morgan. "Expedition to Grand River, Canada for Indian Relics, Oct. 28, 1850." Typed manuscript given to Ian Kenyon by Elizabeth Tooker in June 1984.

146 Frank G. Speck. *The Celestial Bear Comes Down to Earth: The Bear Sacrifice Ceremony of the Munsee-Mahican in Canada as Related by Nekatcit* (Reading, Penn.: Reading Public Museum and Art Gallery, 1945).

147 Frank G. Speck. *The Tutelo Spirit Adoption Ceremony: Reclothing the Living in the Name of the Dead* (Harrisburg: Pennsylvania Historical Commission, 1942).

148 State Historical Society of Wisconsin (Madison), Brant Miscellanies, Lyman Draper Collection, Series F, Vol. 13, p. 29.

149 David Boyle. *The Pagan Iroquois: Archaeological Report of the Minister of Education 1898* (Toronto: Minister of Education, 1898).

150 Patrick Campbell, *Travels in the Interior Inhabited Parts of North America in the Years 1791 and 1792* (Toronto: Champlain Society, 1937, reprint of 1793 edition, with annotations).

151 J. Ross Robertson. *The Diary of Mrs. John Graves Simcoe* (Toronto: William Briggs, 1911).

152 AO. Thorburn Papers, 1845–1862. Diaries, Six Nations Indians.

153 AO. Thorburn Papers, Box 3: v. Diaries 1–20, 1844–1851, Superintendent Six Nations Indians, Number 2: 9 February 1845 to 10 September 1845, Friday 11 July 1845.

154 Ibid. Diary No. 12: 1 March 1849; 21 June 1849; 22 May 1849.

155 Toronto Reference Library, Baldwin Room. William Nelles Accounts and Militia Papers 1792–1837, Accession number S111.

156 NA. RG 10, Vols. 896–906. Accounts, Six Nations Superintendency, 1844–1880.

157 http://www.Cyndislist.com/native.htm

158 New York State Library. Records of the Dutch Reformed Church of Albany, New York 1683–1809, Church Records Collection, Box 1, Accession Number SC17568.

159 Church of Jesus Christ of Latter Day Saints. Records of the First Reformed Church at Schenectady, N.Y. 1683–1784, LDS microfilm 0534207. This item is in the permanent collection of the LDS Family History Centre in Hamilton.

160 Society for the Propagation of the Gospel in Foreign Parts (London, England). Letterbooks 1702–1737, Series A, Vol. 8, pp. 257, 304–305; Vol. 9, p. 227; Vol. 10, p. 190, 219; Vol. 11, pp. 355–356; Vol. 12, p. 411; Vol. 13, pp. 326–327, 337, 487. They are found on microfilm at McMaster University, call number BV 2500.A6L.

161 Rev. Henry Barclay. Register of Marriages, Baptisms, Communicants, and Burials Among the Mohawk Indians, 26 January 1735 to 16 February 1746. Transcripts are available at the Montgomery County Archives, Fonda, New York. See the Appendix.

162 Rev. John Ogilvie. A Register of Indian Children, 22 April 1750 to 11 February 1759. Transcripts are available at the Archives of the State of New York, Albany.

163 Arthur C.M. Kelly. *Baptism Record St. Paul's Lutheran Church, Schoharie, New York 1728–1899* (Rhinebeck, N.Y.: Arthur C.M. Kelly, 1977).

164 Arthur C.M. Kelly. *Baptism Record of the Schoharie Reformed Church, Schoharie, New York 1731–1894* (Rhinebeck, N.Y.: Arthur C.M. Kelly, 1977).

165 Arthur C.M. Kelly. *Baptism Record of Caughnawaga Reformed Church, Fonda, New York 1758–1899* (Rhinebeck, N.Y.: Arthur C.M. Kelly, 1985).

166 Barbara Sivertsen. *Turtles, Wolves and Bears: A Mohawk Family History* (Bowie, MD: Heritage Books, 1996).

167 New York Historical Society. Evert Wendell Indian Account Book 1695–1726, (microfilm 71). The translation of these documents from the original Dutch is extremely hard to decipher, since the translator's system of organization is obscure, and he used a form of shorthand to record the information.

168 Fort Johnson Archives. Fort Johnson, Tribes Hill, New York. Indian book for Jelles Fonda at Cachnewago 1763 April (1752–1763), MSS 1-647.

169 Cornell University Library MSS and Archives. Colonial Account Book, Mohawk Co., Jelles Fonda (1755–1777) (microfilm 903). Another copy is available at the New York State Library, Albany (microfilm A-FM32).

170 James Sullivan et al., eds. *The Papers of Sir William Johnson*. 13 Vols. (Albany: State University of New York, 1921–1965).

171 NA. RG 10, Vol. 113, "Deed from Sachems principal Chiefs and Warriors of the Six Nation Indians residing at the Grand River to Joseph Young," 25 April 1838, pp. 511–513 (microfilm C-11477).

172 Inez Brant-Leonard and Henry Townley Brant. *The Brant-Overlin Saga* (San Jose, CA: Willow Glen Press, 1953).

173 Newhouse.

174 Julia L. Jamieson. *The Mohawk Language*. 3 pamphlets (Jarvis, Ont.: Record Print, 1958). Copies are available at WCC.

175 Shimony, pp. 22–24.

176 Faux.

177 NA. RG 10, Vol. 814, Receipt from John Young chief to William Cook, 4 October 1845, p. 370.

178 Ibid. Receipt from William Young chief to William Cook, 27 December 1845, p. 363.

179 Ibid. Receipt from William Young chief to William Cook, 27 December 1845, p. 363.

180 Ibid. Receipt from Gaiundahe to William Cook, 24 June 1847, p. 366.

181 NA. RG 10, Vol. 898, "Six Nations Indians in Acct with H.A. Van Sickle, Onondaga Ont., 1875 and 1876," p. 120.

Index

Page references in *italic* type indicate case studies. Page references in **bold** type refer to illustrations. Where information about a woman's surname is not given, she has been indexed under her first name. Keep in mind that spelling of names used to vary considerably. A knowledge of phonetics and some imagination will help you find the name you seek.